Life Is a Road,
It's About the Ride

Other books in the *Life Is a Road* series:

Life Is a Road, the Soul Is a Motorcycle

Life Is a Road, Get On it and Ride!

Life Is a Road, Ride It Hard!

Life Is a Road, It's About the Ride

Daniel Meyer

Storm Rider Press
www.stormriderpress.com

Life Is a Road, It's About the Ride

ISBN: 978-0-6151-3850-3

Visit
www.lifeisaroad.com

www.stormriderpress.com

For friends in far away places.

I will love the light for it shows me the way,
yet I will endure the darkness because it shows me the stars.
                                                    —*Og Mandino*

Contents

Acknowledgements

I once again have to express my deepest thanks to my friends Ron Lee and Dan Peters. I am in absolute awe at their talents.

Ron's wonderful illustrations and Dan's gorgeous covers truly capture the spirit of the *Life Is a Road* series, and I appreciate their efforts and dedication.

To my friends and supporters in the on-line community, know that it's only with your help any of this is possible. The early support and encouragement of valkyrieriders.com, xs11.com, bigbikeriders.com, and others encouraged me to publish in the first place. The Internet is changing the way the book publishing industry works, and I'm right in the middle of the revolution. For that, I thank you.

For all my friends, know that this, my, world simply would not exist without you. Keep loving. Keep riding. Keep learning. Keep *living*.

I'll see you on the road.

Introduction

"Why do you do it?"

Shivering and clutching my extra large cup of coffee gingerly between my stone cold, unfeeling hands, I slowly turned from staring out the window to face the convenience store clerk. The young, pretty, sandy-haired girl looked at me from across the counter with an expression of polite interest while I carefully considered my answer. To buy myself a little more time I took a few sips of the steaming creamy beverage.

There was no use pretending that I didn't know what she was asking about. The weather had turned on me and I'd been caught out unprepared. This Texas-bred boy was slowly freezing despite donning all the riding gear I had stashed on the big Valkyrie motorcycle. After fueling I'd stumbled into the store and my hands were shaking so bad she'd had to help me pour the coffee. She'd also had to add the sugar and cream…I couldn't even grasp the small packages, much less tear them open. I'd been riding in the freezing misty conditions for hours, and right now I just wanted, intensely, desperately, to get home.

I turned back to the window. Looking through my own reflection, the cold misty evening outside was cruel and repelling. This night's conditions were going to be absolutely brutal. I shivered violently and wondered if maybe, just maybe, this could be the time I simply wouldn't make it. Home was still an awfully long way away.

Why do I do it? Yah. Good question. Right then I was wondering that myself.

When I started writing the *Life Is a Road* series, I hoped to include stories that helped to answer the question of: "Why ride?" For a time I thought I'd succeeded, but then found the occasion to wonder if I really had. How could it be possible that I had answered that question, or even attempted to answer that question, when many times I wasn't sure of the answer myself?

I ride tens of thousands of miles every year, and have experienced extremes of the fantastical and the mundane, as well as everything in between. I've seen beautiful and stunning landscapes that could truly take my breath away, and just as often, I've ridden through hostile and forbidding places that seem to go on forever.

Folks often ask me why I choose to include certain stories, and then completely fail to even write down others. The answer's not clear. Some places, some people, some *rides* find a place in my memory. My experiences, both tragic and amazing write themselves into my soul long before they find themselves being put to paper. The tragic ones I used to write down and then shred. I suppose I was hoping this in some way would help me purge them from my experience...cleanse them from my soul.

That would be the easy way. Yeah, I know, the easy way seldom works. In the end, we are the sum of our experiences. All of them, good, bad, magical, and mundane, make us what we are and help determine what we can become. We can't hide from our past.

In this volume I've chosen a series of short stories I hope help to illustrate that.

The clerk was waiting. Despite all my experience, despite all those rides, right then, standing there, I found myself completely unable to answer what for me should be a simple question. I looked out at the cold and hostile wind-swept world, lonely, uncertain, and shaking from the cold, and simply wondered *why*.

I glanced at the heavy cruiser and even in the gray light and covered with road-grime she still seemed to call for me. The trees across the road whipped in the wind and a smattering of sleet rattled and skipped across the parking lot. The windows of the store shook in the moaning wind and distorted my reflection. It was cold. It was ugly. It was brutal. But it was time.

I. Simply. Had. To. Ride.

I turned to the young lady, crunching my now empty coffee cup and tossing it in the trash. She was eyeing me closely. Hers had not been an idle question and I was taken aback that I didn't have a ready answer for her.

My mouth worked. The windows rattled, as the sleet, heavier now, blew under the canopy to bounce off them. I looked up sharply at the noise. I'd have to work hard to get south before the roads got too bad to navigate the big machine on. That would be a challenge, but already my heart quickened, looking forward to the prospect.

It is the experience that drives me. Excitement, passion and lust for the journey are parts of my core. I learned long ago that life is a road, and it's how we travel that road and what we see and do along it that define us, not some intended destination at the end of it. It's really not about life—it's not about getting there. It's about *living*—it's about what we do along the way. I smiled. Yeah. That's it. I *did* know.

I pushed open the door and winced at the cold blast of air that cascaded into store. I had an answer for her, but I wasn't sure what she'd make of it. Why do I do it? As I forced my way into the harsh, darkening, windswept evening I stopped and said over my shoulder with a grin, "It's about the ride babe. It's all about the ride."

Life is a road. Live. Ride. See. *Fly*.

Are you ready?

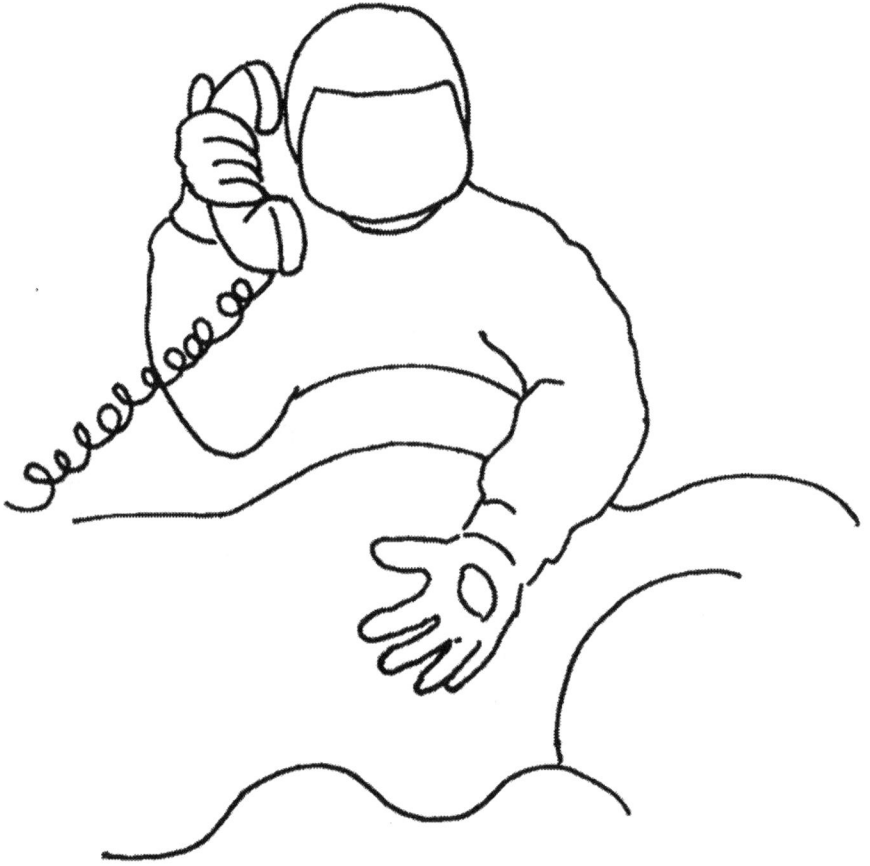

The Call

It's all connected...past, present, and future. The light...and no matter how much we sometimes wish it wasn't...the dark, are a part of who we are and what we can become. I know this. Coming to terms with it however, is a story all its own.

Part One—A Call for Help

Drifting high on the swirling currents, I felt the chest muscles rippling as sweeping wings carried me aloft. Blood pumping through massive arteries bore oxygen gleaned from the rarified air by powerful lungs. A furnace...an engine of infinite power and complexity, a man, a mount, and strangely something much more than all, the Dragon soared effortlessly through the night.

    Minor alterations, muscles tensed, sinews relaxed. A glance, subtle movements...and the flight changed. Almost randomly or at a whim, entire worlds slide by. Realities distort as the beast plummets nearly to its destruction, only to scream in joyous ecstasy and climb back to the heights—simply to do it all over again. It is chaos unleashed to any observing, but actually tightly, precisely controlled— a dance of intricate design, influenced only by the dancers, the flowing passion, and the stars above.

    And then there's the music...

The dance is accompanied by deep, glorious, intricate harmony that emanates from the power of the universe itself...or perhaps it comes from deep in the soul. There is very little difference between the two at the moment.

Overwhelmed with the beauty and passion of it, so caught up in the gestalt, so absorbed by the music, I didn't understand when the first ice-cold flash of pain threatened to spin me into unconsciousness. It happened so fast I wasn't sure it was really even there.

The second slashing white-hot burst of agony left absolutely no doubt.

***

I was dreaming and I knew it. I've done it before. In point of fact, I do it all the time. They are inevitably...*interesting*. This time something was different.

Some believe dreams are the subconscious's way to organize extra sensory input that cannot be processed during waking hours. Basically the five senses, and a probably more than a few extra ones for good measure, are taking in far more information than can be comprehended in real-time. Rather than losing the extra data, the brain shuttles it off to a buffer and then as time permits, processes the information. It discards meaningless data, but should it find a pattern or meaning, shunts the processed bits of information back to the conscious mind.

Those bits may come as strong feelings, or perhaps intuition or simply a vague unease. Extreme cases may hear voices, suddenly "remember" something, or maybe even experience a vision. If we are asleep, we call it dreaming. If we are awake, we call it madness.

***

Flying and free. The clean air clearing my head of old pains. A down-sweep of wings. Heady joy found simply soaring and diving. The taste of the air...the texture of the currents. Oh the POWER!

Lost in the purity of the experience, completely absorbed, it was some time before I realized that I was not the one in control. Uneasily I recalled the pain felt earlier. What could that mean?

A minor jolt; some small pain; a desired correction that I couldn't make happen; All added up to make me realize the truth. Although enticingly familiar, this was not my dream. This was somebody else's flight...I was simply along for the ride. At once I was fearful and fascinated. Why was I here? Whose experience was I sharing? How? Where would it take me? Nothing was clear.

Movement above us. A threat? Failure to react. "I" could see it, why couldn't "we"? A feeling of impending doom. My warnings unheeded. I cried out in vain, finally understanding that in this place, in this other person's dream, I had absolutely no influence.

A flash. A noise. I screamed as intense pain ripped across my soul. Blinded by the agony, ripped apart, the Dragon fell into the chaos. No longer able to distinguish myself as a separate entity, I fell with it. Waves of pain overwhelmed our senses. Angry colors played across our vision. Death reached for us. Tortured beyond endurance, we welcomed it.

"Wait!" My small voice cried out. "It's not time!" Still, we fell, no longer even struggling, longing for the end.

My tortured mind began to comprehend that if I perished in this place, it would somehow mean death in my own world as well.

"Fight, damn you!" I screamed, but there was no consciousness left to answer me. That actually made it easier. The Dragon was nearly gone and that gave me some measure of control.

A Herculean effort, a twist, and abruptly I ripped away from the death and pain. Plummeting away from the sundered Dragon, paralyzed by the loss, I could only fall...and weep. What had happened here?

***

I cried out as I fell from the high bed, smashing my head on the bedside table as I crashed to the floor. A lamp fell on me and I heard glass breaking. Throwing off the blankets and stray pillows that had fallen with me, I lurched for the bathroom, half crawling, half running, barely making it before skidding to my knees and retching. Minutes went by before I could catch my breath. Of its own accord my head was flailing around and I realized I was still looking for *The Dragon*, but all I could see was red with black patches swimming across my vision. That only spawned another round of retching and I forced my eyes closed. The remembered pain nearly overwhelmed me.

By feel I stumbled into the shower and spun the faucet handles, sloppily adjusting the water as hot and as hard as I could stand it. I was sobbing uncontrollably from the pain and loss of the dream and I had to concentrate to get a full breath in between the racking sobs. The hot jets and soothing steam slowly returned me to the real world and calmed my spasms. Finally, mostly in control of myself, I was able to gasp, "Oh my god!" and slowly open my eyes.

"What the hell was that about?" I shouted to the walls. I wasn't expecting any answers. I certainly didn't know and only the two cats were in the house. The wife had gone on a vacation to see her parents and I wasn't expecting her back for at least another week. That was a relief, because as much as I desperately needed to hold somebody...*anybody*...I couldn't explain this to myself, much less my wife. What would I have said to her?

The stinging on my scalp and the traces of red washing down the drain with the shower water brought me the rest of the way into reality. I put my hand to my head and felt around. The cut was bleeding profusely and there was already a large bump. I pulled a washcloth from the rack and pressed it hard against the wound. I'd get some ice for it later.

All too soon the hot water began to run out. I had been thinking long and hard about the dream and what I had carried away from it. For once, my intuition was failing me completely. I had a strong sense of foreboding and loss, yet no hint of *why* or what I should do. I shut off the shower and as I looked at the chaos in the bedroom, resolved to make some phone calls.

***

The mess was cleaned up and I was tucked into my warm bed trying to sleep. The cats had been cowering under the couch, but once I cleaned up the blood and coaxed them out, they had contentedly curled up beside me on the bed. Both were asleep and purring gently and I found I envied them.

Several phone calls had assured me that close friends and family were all accounted for, yet still I could not shake the atmosphere of loss and foreboding. Something was wrong. As I fell into an uneasy sleep I wondered how long I would have to wait to find out what.

Five nights would pass by before I had my answer.

***

I knew when the phone rang that it was bad news. Nothing good ever comes from a two AM phone call.

I answered on the third ring. "Hello?"

There was no reply, but there was a connection. I could hear a breath, almost a sigh. I have a strong sense about these things and waited patiently. Somebody was deciding something.

Finally. Hesitatingly. "Daniel?"

I recognized the voice. I could think of no reason *she* would ever call me. I could think of several reasons why she wouldn't though. "She hates me" would be high on that list.

I blinked a couple times before answering, trying to collect my thoughts. "Yeah?"

"Daniel, I'm not...well...you know I wouldn't call you."

That was an understatement but there was no point in antagonizing her. I kept my voice cool and even. "Yes, I know." I took a breath. "Yet here we are."

She sighed, "*He* needs your help."

There are lots of people in this world I'll help out. Friends and family...and even strangers can ask for help and usually get it. It may be on my schedule, or terms...or I may ask all sorts of embarrassing questions, but I'll help if I can.

That said, there is another category of "help". There are people in this world that I will lay down my life for. People that can call and I'll give them anything, anywhere, anytime...help them with anything...without comment or question. Bonds forged so tightly that time, distance, or arguments simply cannot break them. Bonds forged clawing our way out of several hells, and sealed with blood. Lives saved, sacrifices made, and debts repaid so many times that it was no longer possible to make an accounting. With these people, so deep is the bond, that there is no need...or desire to understand the complicated web of experiences that bind us. Those people are few.

There are maybe two of them on the planet. *She* was not one of them, even by extension. *He* was.

I took a deep breath and kept my voice even, "Then *he'd* better ask me for it." I harbored no animosity for her at all. She hated me, yes, but I didn't hate her. She simply didn't have the right to ask and I couldn't picture the circumstances where she would.

"I…well…you," she stopped and took a breath. My foreboding from the nightmare I'd had days before clicked into place. I knew what she was going to say before she said it, but waited for it just the same. Her voice wavered, "He can't ask you. He's dead."

Yah. That would about do it.

She said it in a rush, "He was killed in a motorcycle accident five nights ago." I could hear anger in her voice.

Of course he was. *Damn.*

I closed my eyes and held the phone receiver against my forehead, the cool plastic soothing to the touch despite the crunching and crackling noises it was somehow making. I knew she was telling the truth. I had probably known it when I first heard her voice.

Those people are few. There used to be more. And now there was only one. *Damn.*

"I'm coming." I hung up the phone. The crushed plastic handset fell apart in the cradle and I looked dully at the blood streaming from the cuts in my hand.

Damn.

I looked at the empty place in the bed beside me and for once I was glad I was sleeping alone. The women in my life have always been happier to believe that there was no…*before.* My past before them has always been best left unexplored. Questions are answered, I've little to hide, but for the most part, they've been content not to know. Uncomfortable subjects, if they ever come up, are met with a not-too-subtle subject change and never revisited. They prefer it if strong past influences simply don't exist. This one was complicated, with portions of it deep and dark. Old lovers, old loyalties, dark moments, and joy beyond reckoning. Parts I would expose, but others I couldn't talk about…even with my wife. They could only be discussed with one other…and now he was dead. Secrets to the grave…*pain far beyond.*

I had to go, and was relieved not to have to try to explain *why* to the woman I love. It would take time I couldn't spare. Besides, I've been here before. It had cost me dearly then.

Ten minutes later I was northbound on *The Dragon*, and fast. The big machine was rumbling and warm beneath me, yet the cold night air was chilling me despite my heavy leather jacket. The discomfort was a welcome distraction. Right now I needed to ride more than I needed to think. My grief, if it ever came, would have to wait. Right now all I had was wonder. What could he want of me from beyond the grave, and just how was he asking? I snarled and twisted the throttle to its stop. The big bike wailed its lonely scream as we sailed into the night.

Twelve hours in the saddle. Nearly 900 miles traveled. I got off the big Valkyrie cruiser and entered the house uninvited, shaking with cold and exhaustion. They were waiting for me in the living room when I arrived.

She was there, of course, as well as an older man I did not recognize. Another, younger man stood by her side and although I did not recognize him personally, I knew his type. His look and bearing labeled him a security man, or perhaps a cop. Either way, in this circumstance, he was hired muscle. I suppressed a grin. Even after all this time of being with *him*, she still did not know me…either my integrity, or what I am capable of under the right circumstances. Had she known the first, she would not have bothered with the muscle. Had she known the second, she would have brought a whole lot more.

The older man had the answers. Turned out he was a lawyer. He was almost smiling when he said, "I have the will…and some papers." There was nothing mean spirited or deceitful in his eyes. He seemed relieved to see me.

I kept my eyes focused on his as I pointed at the hired muscle. "Is he relevant?"

"No." There was just the trace of a grin, only for a moment.

I turned to the person in question. "You, leave. Now."

"Now just a minute…" she had started to object but stopped when she saw my face.

I ignored her, watching the goon carefully. If he was going to do something stupid, now was when he'd do it. He was looking at each of us in turn—the girl, the lawyer, and then me. His gaze lingered longest on mine, his arms poised for action. I narrowed my eyes and barely shook my head, just once. I would give no other warning. Something had hardened in me during the long ride and I was spoiling for a fight. It would not be pretty or nice if it got started. He was smarter than he looked. He relaxed perceptibly, shrugged, and walked out of the room.

Since nobody was offering, I stomped off to the kitchen to find the makings for some coffee, hoping to shake the chill from the long ride off. In a few minutes I had a steaming pot ready and I brought enough back for everybody, as well as cups and trimmings. I unceremoniously deposited it on the coffee table, selected a comfortable chair, sat down, and waited, sipping my coffee and munching some cookies I'd found. I said nothing. They had been waiting on me.

They'd get started when they were damn good and ready.

Part 2—A Message from the Past

I sat quietly in my chair, sipping coffee and wondering. The past slipped into and out of focus. Old feelings, old passions, boiled and seethed under the surface. Things could have been very different.

The girl...*her*...was Karen, and I stared unabashedly. There was anger in her eyes when she saw I was watching but shortly she blushed and looked away. Curvy, trim, redheaded, and green-eyed, she was still as beautiful as I remembered her. Redheads are a weakness of mine, but I found it telling that now I felt no attraction for her at all. There is more to desire than physical appearance...and I suppose I knew what her soul looked like. In truth I felt nothing. Complete indifference. I am a passionate man. Indifference is a rare thing for me when there is a woman in the room.

Besides, I'd had her long ago. I'd thought she was mine, then.

The dead man that had called me here...*He*...was Jack. Jack had done well, after our history...after our...death...and life together. Seeking solitude to heal his wounds, he had taken up trucking, and had driven for a major discount retailer back when they were small and aggressively expanding. Capital had run short and they had drastically cut the pay, making up the difference in leveraged company stock. Most of the drivers had left. Jack, enjoying the isolated life and knowing the basics of compounding mathematics, had not. Several years later he looked at the large number of zeros that had accumulated on the end of his banking balance and promptly retired.

We seldom saw each other. The bonds we shared did not require it, and the experiences we had shared made it painful. Then came the day he needed help and called me. I went, of course. I didn't even ask why beyond the needed information concerning who...or what...I should bring along.

"Armed?"

"Not necessary."

"I'm on the way," was my simple reply. Karen was my girlfriend at the time and had been astonished, then outraged. Not ten words had passed between Jack and I on the phone, and now I was leaving. I couldn't even tell her why other than that I was going to help an old friend. She had insisted that I not go, and when I was preparing to leave anyway, had offered herself in a way I particularly enjoyed, simply to distract me from my task and get her way.

It is difficult to leave a gorgeous, green-eyed redhead lying naked across the couch in the living room, but it can be done. Her insistence that I ignore my friend's call for help actually made it easier. A truly beautiful woman would not have asked me for that.

It was the beginning of the end of Karen and I. *Hell hath no fury* and all that. Life…and death…had conditioned me to not worry about the small things, and I often have trouble understanding others when they do. It mattered to Karen that in my friend I had something. Something she could not understand. Something that was not hers. Something she could not control.

Something she could not take.

The sad truth of the matter is that if Karen could have understood what Jack and I had, she would not have wanted it. She would not have tried to interfere. Jack and I both would have been far happier had we never met each other, but often we don't get to choose our own path. Sometimes the world can be dark and cruel. Sometimes we must fight, no matter the cost.

Sometimes demons walk the earth, and men look the other way. Some of us don't, perhaps we can't, and for us, sometimes the cost is terribly high.

I was only gone two days, but things were different when I got home. Colder. More often than not I was back to sleeping alone, which, knowing how tenuous life can be, I hated with a loathing beyond description. Of course the alternative was not for me either. Sex is a thing to be freely given, not a weapon, never a bribe to get your way. Powerful it is…a basic magic of the human soul…and is a very special thing when wielded properly, but a bribe? A payment? It simply won't work that way on me. Life might have been much simpler if it could.

Weeks passed, but the day came when she tried to get her way again. Jack was in town and he and some of my other, local friends were visiting me at the house. This was a rare thing. Perhaps some of our trauma was fading and our lives could normalize a bit. Perhaps the memories were stale enough to begin to lose influence. They say time heals all wounds. I wasn't really sure I believed that, but thought it was worth a try.

The typical bachelor, my cupboard was bare and I had to step out for supplies. My other friends were frequent guests and knew I was a moderate drinker. Correctly figuring I was bound to screw up any decent beer run, they took off on one of their own.

When I returned, only Karen's car was in the drive. It had not been there when I left. I guessed what my other friends were about and figured Karen and I would have some time. I had not seen her for several days and was looking forward to a visit with her. When everybody got back, it would be fun to introduce her around. *That* turned out not to be necessary. Pity.

Turned out that Karen had shown up just as the other foraging party was getting organized, so she had shooed them on their way, leaving only her and Jack to get acquainted. When I returned, I had unloaded the groceries into the house, and then wandered to my bedroom, hoping to find her waiting for me.

Jack and Karen were there, together. I'm not even sure I was terribly surprised. When I entered the room, Karen had thrown back the covers and said something rehearsed and dramatic about betrayal, passion, and how I couldn't trust a friend. Jack's face had registered only confusion.

It had been a plan. Karen's plan. And it had failed…at least to a point. She had counted on my anger and passion overwhelming my…less animal…senses. They didn't. She thought I would see clearly that this was Jack's fault. Jack's betrayal. It might have worked if she had seduced one of my other friends. She didn't want some other friend. She wanted Jack. She thought by seducing him she could drive something between Jack and I.

She didn't understand the history…had no clue what we had suffered together…what we had defeated…and at what cost. She did not know that the word "friend" didn't really describe Jack and I. She had missed the concept that we were not really friends at all, but rather brothers in all but blood…that our lives had been held in each other's hands. We were friends only because we survived. We were friends only because there was no other word for it.

The scene was clear. She had known about Jack. Jack had not known about her. My mistake I guess. Looking at her lying there naked and proud, smelling the sex in the room, seeing her so obviously and freshly used by another, *knowing* she had orchestrated this...*even then* my physical desire gave a sharp response. Just a little too late, I finally understood.

I realized that this was the type of woman that wars had been fought for. She was physically gorgeous, erotic, and simply dripped sexuality. She possessed, in spades, all the magic of a woman. What's more she understood that magic at a purely mechanical level. She had the will to use that gift to coerce men into doing her bidding. She didn't love. She *bought*. I hadn't been responding correctly, my heart hadn't been for sale, so she was on to another, and with a bonus— hurting me as well. It's too bad she didn't understand she couldn't buy my heart because I'd already given it to her.

I hadn't expected this and Jack had no clue who she was. Had he known, he would not have let her seduce him, and being who he was, would have told me of the attempt later. Not knowing, he'd had no reason to resist her, and with no reason, very few would say no to her attentions. I wouldn't. *I hadn't.*

I had paused in the doorway long enough to take all this in, then smiled, winked at Jack, and said, "Hey! Good going buddy! Man, she IS hot!" At this, Karen, who had willingly and enthusiastically given herself to me in far more exposed positions, had actually pulled the covers back over herself and blushed.

I whistled at her, nodded appreciatively, and said cheerfully, "Oh, don't mind me. You two have fun, and look me up when you're done. I'll feed you."

I gave Jack a "thumbs up" and pulled the door closed.

***

A simple but very tasty stew was in the crock. Hot, crisp French bread topped with butter, garlic, and bubbling cheddar cheese was just out of the broiler. Dips and chips were on the table. Cold beer and other beverages were making the rounds, with plenty of surplus in the fridge. Music was playing at one end of the house, and sci-fi movies were showing at the other. Without a word to me Karen had left shortly after my interruption, but the rest of my friends had arrived immediately afterwards. The party was in full swing.

Jack and I talked. He's not stupid and had realized there was more going on than met the eye, but life is often complicated that way. I wasn't angry at all. Actually, I was relieved. Karen and I had been done for some time. I just hadn't known it. Jack wanted to see her again. I found that I didn't care. I just hoped he knew what he was getting into. Maybe she could at least quell his nightmares as she had mine. She was good at that at least. Female magic works wonders on tortured men's souls.

They were married a few months later. Her plan had backfired in a way. She had fallen for him and still failed to drive our bond apart, even though Jack and I rarely spoke. She didn't understand this, and whatever emotion she had ever harbored for me, she simply turned into hate. I didn't sweat it. Life goes on, and I was well into "on" with mine. Complicated. Yeah. That's it.

***

They had been happy. So had I. *So was I.* But now he was dead. I glanced at the lawyer and wondered just what Jack had asked of me. Ashamed of myself, I wondered how dearly it would cost me this time.

I sat in my chair, sipped my coffee, and stared at Karen. She stared fixedly at the wall. Her face made it clear. Even in her grief, she couldn't lose her hate. Pity. She'd be so much prettier without hate.

Finally the lawyer broke the uneasy silence as he handed me an envelope, "This is for you, and is the certified accounting of the estate." This was simplified of course. There were still probate issues to deal with and current appraisals on the real property, but this was the starting point.

Still watching Karen, I slipped a finger under the flap, slit it open, and only when I had the letter unfolded in my hand, dropped my eyes and examined the figure on the paper. I then did a double take. Jack had done VERY well. Better than I had expected by several sets of zeros. Better than I had. *Better than I dreamed.*

The lawyer spoke to me again. "The will is pretty simple. You get all the cash and real property." At this Karen sobbed, but did not appear surprised. I suppose she couldn't have been. In my home state at least, if the spouse is not the primary beneficiary, he/she must have been shown and signed the will. I turned my attention back to the lawyer as he spoke again, "Karen gets her personal property and lifetime occupancy of the house, which as part of the estate you now own."

I blinked. I hadn't expected anything remotely like this. It didn't make sense. There had to be more to it. I was still digesting the implications when the lawyer asked Karen to step out of the room. Somehow she had realized...or been convinced that her fate was in other's hands. She left without complaint.

He handed me another envelope. "Jack had several personal requests for you."

I opened it and sat back in my chair to read. Ah, so that was it. Item one was a delivery I needed to make, and a bit of a surprise, but the rest of the list was more what I had expected. Shortly I raised one eyebrow and looked at the lawyer. "You've seen this?"

"Yes." He looked at me expectantly.

"Then arrange it."

"You do realize it's not in any way legally binding."

"Arrange it."

He smiled. "It's already done. I just need your signature and to arrange for the delivery items."

That was a hint. The delivery was still a mystery, but I began to comprehend just what it was that Jack was up to...just what it was he was trying to say.

The lawyer handed me a clipboard. A line was clearly highlighted for my signature. Jack's was on the line right above it. I scanned the text and then signed without hesitation and handed it back.

He took the clipboard and shook my hand as he said, "You sir, are an honorable man."

I thought of the passion of youth, the dollar figure on the piece of paper, and the pain and darkness of parts of my past. I thought of my wife, friend, and lover in my present, and recalled the past vision of a naked redhead lying across my couch. The same redhead I could still smell in this room. The one that had been mine.

My thoughts darkly male, I found myself wondering if he was right.

***

The big cruiser idling beneath me, I looked into the evening sky and pondered the weather. This was not the ideal time of year for long, cross-country motorcycle journeys. I'm not at all fond of the cold, and it certainly was that, but any kind of freezing precipitation can spell disaster or delay for a motorcyclist. I was almost certain to run into sleet or snow in some of the mountain passes.

There had been three requests on that piece of paper, the first two of which required travel.

One was a delivery to a specific person. I didn't really have to use the motorcycle for that. But the other errand required it. That was an understanding, unspoken and from long ago, but no less strong…no less binding. The first was on the way to the other. Both were a very long way away. Fifteen hundred miles at a guess, and there were mountains between the targets and me.

The smart thing to do would be to go home and grab the truck. The big Dodge could handle anything thrown at it and was the more suitable vehicle for the possible weather to be found along my route this time of year. On a whim I rapidly refigured the journey, mentally adding nearly 300 miles to let me stick to the southern route. Even at that, there were still mountains in the way.

The smart thing. The legal thing. The right thing. They are not always the same. Sometimes they are not even close.

I took a deep breath and held it a moment, hoping for inspiration. It didn't come. My instincts were screaming to take the bike. That made no sense, but sometimes instinct is all I've got.

"Screw it." The honorable thing was to take the bike. There just wasn't any getting around that. For some reason the instinct strongly agreed. I twisted the throttle and roared into the advancing sunset.

***

Many hours later, I found myself shivering and alone, on foot and limping along the frozen, slushy road. I was just a couple miles from my first target. I had a heavy duffle bag slung across my back. One glove was torn, and the right leg of my jeans was ripped from the ankle to the knee. The bleeding on the leg had been minor and already stopped, but the deep gouges on the boot gave an additional and ominous hint of recent events.

I kicked at the icy road and winced at the stinging sensation in my very cold feet. The frozen landscape was isolated and beautiful, but I grimly reflected that surprise weather systems and snowplow scheduling would rate higher in my consideration should I embark on any future spur-of-the-moment, winter, cross-country motorcycle journeys.

Predawn light was just beginning to illuminate the landscape and I paused to admire the astounding view. My breathing was heavy, trying to pull enough oxygen from the high altitude air. I watched the cloud of fog billow each time I exhaled. My overwhelming thought was only that I really, *really* should have taken the truck…or maybe the redhead.

I had done the honorable thing, and I wasn't finished. I was still doing the honorable thing. Yeah.

I kicked again at the frozen road and resumed walking, mumbling with a grin, "Sometimes honor sucks."

Yeah. Sometimes it does at that.

Part 3—Obligations

The small cluster of modest houses looked well kept. Situated on one side of the minor state highway, all of them backed up to heavily wooded Forest Service property. The other side of the road fell off into a gently sloped meadow. In the dawn light the forest was dark and inviting, the meadow white and glistening with the snow. It was all so unlike the huge gash of concrete and steel that is the city I live in. I took a deep breath of the crisp, clean air. Life on the mountain. Wow!

I glanced at the sheaf of papers the lawyer had given me, verifying the house I wanted. There could be no mistake. The lawyer was coolly competent. In my dealings with him he had been completely prepared, intrinsically aware of the "right" thing, and mysteriously appearing exactly when, and only when he was needed.

The instructions for the delivery comprised a full-color set of laminated maps, each in the series very detailed and a closer zoom on the area. They were bound by a single ring in the corner and arranged in order. They were almost the perfect size for the map pocket in my tank bag. The first in the series had been countrywide in scale; the last was the exact block I now stood on. The very last page was a color photograph of the house. Underneath the photo was the actual address and phone numbers and a smaller photo of the woman I was to make the delivery to.

Through, complete, intuitive, and flawless. I chuckled to myself. It was all rather fundamentally unlike my usual methods of navigation (point 'er west and gun the throttle). One similarity though…I still didn't know why I was coming here. I mean, I had a delivery to make, and I would carry that out, I even had a very solid idea what I was carrying, but I still had no clue as to why. Why her? Why here?

I had reservations about showing up in my condition. Most folks would be a bit nervous to find a 300-pound biker-guy clad in a heavy, black-leather jacket (covered in embroidered red dragons nonetheless) standing on their porch. Add torn jeans, a bit of blood and some bruises, as well as the minor detail of the complete lack of a motorcycle, and things just wouldn't add up. Calling would have been the smart thing, but Jack's instructions had been clear on that point. She was not to know I was coming.

There was no point in putting it off. I limped straight up the walk and reached up to knock on the door. Almost before my knuckles touched, the door opened to reveal the woman in the picture. Forty-ish and healthily plump, the blue-eyed brunette was tall enough to look me straight in the eyes despite my six-foot frame. Her broad shoulders matched her height and gave the impression that she was a bit of a tomboy. A terrycloth bathrobe mostly covered her, except it was way too short. Ample breasts, a pronounced curve to her hips, and shapely, muscular legs left no doubt that she was all woman. There was no mistaking the face. This was my target.

Apparently my brain hadn't managed to navigate any further ahead than this. I stared. My mouth worked. I couldn't think of what to say. What do you say? *"Pardon me, but some dead guy from the other side of the country sent me here to deliver something, but I'm not sure exactly what or why?"* or how about, *"Beyond the Grave Delivery Service, sign here please."*

She took her cue from my appearance, silence, and bewildered expression.

"Oh dear. You've been in an accident." She grabbed me by the hand and pulled me inside. "Come in! Sit!"

Folks that live in the small towns are usually friendly and helpful.

Before I knew it I was warming myself by the fire and nursing a cup of hot chocolate. Her rapid-fire questions showed that she had a cool head on her shoulders. "Was there anybody else with you? Are you breathing okay? Anything broken? What day is it?"

"No, yes, no, um...uh..."

I actually had a bit of trouble with that last one. What day? Hell I didn't know. I'd been awake for at least three days, and most of that had been spent riding hard. No sleep, extreme riding, and excessive caffeine can combine to interesting effect. I was pretty wired already and figured with about five more soft-drinks or a couple cups of coffee I ought to be able to just concentrate and teleport myself to my next destination...provided my somewhat fuzzy brain could actually manage to remember just where that was.

"The phones are out. Happens every time we have a storm. We'll have to get the truck out of the garage and get you to the clinic. They can radio for an ambulance if you need one."

I held up my hand. "I'm fine. I just need to warm up a bit. Besides, I really didn't have an accident…well…okay I sort-of had an accident…I did drop my bike…but I…well…three times…the last was the worst…it's okay though, I just…" I abruptly stopped talking. Swallowed.

Jheeze I was a mess. My hands were shaking. I took a deep breath, blinked, shuddered, "Let me start over. Give me a minute." My head hurt. Now was *not* the time to let all this catch up with me.

I looked around the living room a moment. Even as small as it was, hardwood floors, comfortable heavy leather furniture, and the stone fireplace made it a very welcoming place.

Finally I felt up to talking. That didn't mean that I had any idea what to say though. I looked at her, "It's parked at the gas station at the turn off into town."

She stared. "What?"

"My bike. I couldn't ride anymore. The snowplows didn't turn up this way. I fell three times trying in about a block. I was moving pretty good on the last one." I grinned and indicated my torn jeans. "I left the bike at the gas station and walked here."

I blinked. She hadn't been holding the stainless revolver a split-second ago. It wasn't pointed at me…not quite.

Folks that live in small towns can take care of themselves.

"Explain yourself." She was quick; I'll give her that. That little bit of information had told her I wasn't here by accident. I had come to *her*.

I still didn't know how to say it. I eyed the gun, thought a moment. Decided. She would know, or she wouldn't. Simple would probably be best.

"I've a delivery for you, from Jack."

Her eyes betrayed her. Recognition, regret, hope, a little fear. All played out in those deep blue eyes. The color drained out of her face.

"Jack?" the words came out in a rush, "He's not coming here is he? I haven't told *her*. I didn't even know he knew where we were."

"No. He's not coming. He's dead. I'm sorry. He asked me to deliver something to you."

"Dead?" She seemed to go limp.

"Yes. A motorcycle accident." I stood up and took the gun from her unresisting fingers. It was cocked; I carefully released it and set it on the fireplace mantle.

She watched me as I sat back down, and then she slowly sank into the chair across from me. "Strange, him going out that way. He loved motorcycles. How tragic!"

Strange? I'd thought so too. Tragic? I wasn't so sure. A *man* will fight to the bitter end, but when it does come, at least for me, I'd hope I'd find my end quickly and doing something I love. Tragic? I think not. Especially after what Jack had been through. I was one of only a few that could understand that. Relief might be a better word. At least there could be no more nightmares. This was not the place to air my musings though. I just nodded.

The front door banged open and a young lady came bounding in. "Hey Mom!" She saw us sitting in the living room, approached. "Oh, hi!" she actually curtsied to me. She turned to her mom. "I forgot my books. I've got to study some tonight. Dad's going to help me with my paper. He says he'll have me back home by eight o'clock Sunday night." She seemed totally unconcerned about me sitting there and bounced down the hallway and out of sight.

I had caught sight of her face and had instantly known why I was here. She was perhaps seventeen or so. She had her mother's hair and build, but Jacks eyes and jaw were clearly prevalent. This was unmistakably his daughter. Since "Dad" didn't live here and was waiting in the driveway, I knew there was more going on than met the eye. Complicated. Yep. That's life.

Shortly she trotted back into the room carrying a backpack. "Got 'em. Love you Mom!" On her way out the door she hollered, "Oh yeah, phones are out again!"

Slam. Just like that, she was gone. Her interruption had been timely. The enthusiasm and energy of her youth, as well as her light voice and loving message broke the tension in the room. I couldn't help but chuckle and her mother was smiling and wiping a few tears from her face.

I nursed my hot chocolate till it was gone, giving her some time.

Shortly, she was ready. She looked up at me, "You knew Jack?"

"Yes. We went through...a lot...together." I had started to say "hell" but stopped myself. Here was not the time or place.

"Then you know she's his." She looked away.

"Yes," I set my empty cup down on the table. "I didn't before just now. It's in her eyes." I shrugged and smiled. "Life can be messy sometimes."

"I wasn't married yet. Jack came through my town every five weeks. My boyfriend was also an over-the-road driver." She got up quickly and picked up my empty cup. "More hot chocolate?"

"Sure." She needed the break.

From the kitchen she spoke, her clear and slightly husky voice carrying, "She was six before I realized. That's when her face showed it. My boyfriend and I were already married and divorced by then. She looked up at me one day…and I swear…that's the first time I knew."

She came back into the room. "By then it was too late. Jack was already married."

"Yes." A vision of the nude redhead lying across my couch flashed before my eyes and I forced them closed. "Yes."

"He and I were the only ones that knew. My daughter doesn't, and neither does my ex. They love each other, and he's a supporting father. I just can't tell her now. It's not right." She was crying again.

"Complicated." I'd spoken quietly.

"What?"

I looked up at her. "Life." I shrugged. "It's seldom clean and neat. Complicated." I grinned at her. "It's what makes it worth living."

"Yes." She sighed, ready to deal with it. I found I admired her a lot. She was recovering from a series of surprises that would have left many hysterical. "Jack had said he'd put her through college…help out…if he left her in the will, she'll have to know about it, right?"

I took a deep breath. *That's* why I was here.

***

I knew what I was carrying. I just hadn't been sure why. I recalled the way the lawyer had presented me with the items for this delivery. He had handed me an empty duffel bag, and then, one at a time, had handed me 25 rectangular packages. He made sure each was out of my hands and in the duffel before he picked up the next and handed it to me.

"Did you know," he had said to me, "that large cash transactions are effectively illegal in this country?"

I had said nothing.

He handed me the next package. "Any cash changing hands, even between individuals, has to be reported to the IRS and banking authorities if the actual transaction is an amount over $9,999."

"Interesting."

"Records have to be kept. The cash has to be tracked. The intent is to make it difficult for drug dealers and tax evaders."

I shrugged. "Intent, even if it was honorable to start with, is usually the first principle sacrificed when a law is enforced. Usually it simply makes much of the things good men do…illegal…more difficult."

He handed me another. "Large amounts of cash have to be declared when boarding planes, trains, or busses too. Get caught without doing that, and it's effectively forfeit, even if from a legitimate transaction."

"Figures."

He had looked up at me, "I am a very expensive lawyer. Jack has paid me a lot of cash over the years so I would carry out his wishes."

I hefted the inch thick package a moment, put it in the duffel. Nobody would've ever known if one or all of these had disappeared. I looked him in the eyes, repeated his earlier words, "You sir, are an honorable man."

He'd looked at me sharply. "The law presumes there are no honorable men."

"The law presumes too much."

He had smiled as he handed me the last package. "I see that we understand each other."

"That, we do." I zipped the duffel and stuck out my hand. "Goodbye."

He gripped it warmly. "Safe journey."

Yes, I knew why Jack had sent me here.

***

I accepted the cup she was handing me, sipped the sweet warm beverage. My chill was gone. It was time to get on the road. I set the cup on the table. "Your daughter's not in the will. Neither are you. Nobody has to know who Jack was until you feel it's right."

"You know."

I'd draped my jacket on the back of the heavy chair. I reached in it and pulled out the sheaf of maps that had led me here. I held it up, looked a moment, and then flipped it into the fire. Brightly colored flames engulfed it rapidly. "Me? Hell, I don't even know where you live."

She watched it burn. "I don't understand why you're here. What is it you have for me?"

I unzipped the duffel, selected a single package, and passed it to her. "Did you know that large cash transactions are effectively illegal in this country?"

"Is that so?"

I pulled out another. "It's an IRS thing. Records have to be kept. The cash has to be tracked...."

***

Warm, empty handed, and recharged on chocolate, I'd made good time hiking back down the hill. The gas station was open now, and they had duct tape! Cool! Instant jean repair. I would need them more or less intact. It was bloody cold up here and the scrapes had stung terribly in the harsh air. I still had a long way to go.

I had laughed out loud, almost hysterically as I was gassing the bike. One by one they passed. Three snowplows came back and started up the hill into town. Timing. Sheesh.

The Dragon idling beneath me, I sat lightly in the saddle and pondered. I was trying to prepare myself for the next leg of my journey, but shortly, decided there was no way I could. The heavy duffel with my next delivery was tied on my back seat. I had no directions for this one. I didn't need them. I knew exactly where I was going. After all, I'd spent the last two decades routing my trips to avoid the area. I snorted. That was very unlike me, and I hadn't noticed it before.

Carefully I worked the big bike out of the slick parking lot. It wouldn't do to injure my ride or myself any further. As I entered the bigger highway and ran the machine through its gears I also made a snap decision. The next large town I passed through would be serving me a very large breakfast. I held a hand up in front of my face, found it was shaking. I might even catch a motel room and get some sleep. I was pretty wracked out, and some rest would help.

I needed to be at my best where I was going.

I wasn't sure what else I'd find, it'd been over twenty years...

But I knew one thing for sure...

There was at least one gate to Hell at that place.

Part 4—Obstructions for the Living

"What'll you have?"

I blinked and tried to focus, but hard riding and cold winds had done me in. I couldn't read the menu. That can be crippling in a big city or chain restaurant, a menu is required simply so you can say such clever things as, "The rutti-king-bunny-wuzzy-fuzzy breakfast platter, with a side of sunrise fresh orange flavored substitute beverage." Even in the less "cute" places you've got to be able to tell the waitress something like, "A number two," or they end up hopelessly lost and unable to function.

Smaller towns are much simpler. Tell 'em what you want…they'll cook it for you. If you want to keep it simple, just order the special. They'll bring you what they think you're hungry for. A good waitress in a small town will nearly always get this right.

I needed to keep it simple. I didn't feel up to stringing more than a sentence or two together. There'd be no telling what I'd say. Seventy-two hours on cookies, coffee, sodas, and hot chocolate can have that effect. Add hard riding and intense cold, as well as more than a little dread of completing the particular errand I was on, and I was feeling a might bit unpredictable.

I looked up at the matronly waitress. She was watching me with concern. "Frazzled" apparently shows through eventually, no matter how tough I pretend to be.

I dropped my eyes back down to the useless menu. "The 'Special' please." I looked up at her again. She was blurry. "Lots of protein."

She took the menu. It was apparently that transitional morning hour. "Breakfast or lunch?"

"Breakfast. Definitely breakfast."

"You've got it hon. Coffee?"

"Yah. And iced tea. *And* orange juice. Lots of orange juice."

***

The bright and sunny morning had been glorious for riding, even if the freezing temperatures weren't to my liking. Blue skies, clear roads, and light traffic had allowed me to make really good time. I had intended to stop much earlier for a meal and some rest, but once again had lost myself in the riding. Even exhausted, the open road calls to me hard.

Flying, free, alive.

It is difficult for me not to listen.

Running low on gas, I pulled into town to fuel up. Four gallons later I reached for the receipt as it was printing out of the pump, and the next thing I knew, I was on the ground trying to push a half-ton of motorcycle off my left leg.

"What the hell?" I was furious.

I managed to get the bike upright just before the clerk ran out to help. One of the universe's laws about motorcycles is that if you do something stupid, there are always people around to witness the result. Mumbling something about slipping on the ice, I mounted the big cruiser. The clerk glanced down at the pavement and my eyes followed. It was clean and dry. Crud. It was time for some rest.

I rounded on the clerk. "Breakfast! Where's breakfast?" That was about as articulate as I could get at the moment.

He got my meaning. "Two blocks down. A diner. Best place around. You can't miss it."

I had a rather annoying vision of me crashing my Valkyrie right through the front door of the place. *Can't miss it?* I shuddered. "Yah, I'm more than a little worried about that."

***

The waitress had taken good care of me. Almost magically my coffee and tea never seemed to get low. The orange juice was freshly squeezed and cold and she brought it out in a quart mason jar (same as the iced tea "glass"). "The Special" when it arrived was a huge fluffy omelet, stuffed with cheddar cheese and an excellent crumbled sausage I couldn't identify. Venison and pork maybe? I didn't know. I didn't care.

Sides had included two fluffy pancakes that would have made a meal in themselves for a normal appetite. Fresh strawberries and grapes accompanied them and were the perfect touch.

Believe me when I say, a good meal can save your life. This wasn't a good meal…this was a *great* one.

"You are headed south, yes?" the waitress was back on one of her magical coffee filling runs. The mark of a professional waitress, if she hadn't said anything I would have never known she had come by until I noticed the full cup. Good waitresses have some ninja in their background methinks.

I looked up from my meal, "Mmmumph?" Yah, those pancakes were good.

She waved at the television hanging in the corner. I hadn't even noticed it before. The weather report was on, and despite the blue, sunny skies outside, it didn't look good.

"Storm's coming in. They're calling for blizzard conditions in the mountains tonight. That's no place for a motorcycle. You need to get south," she look concerned. "You are going south…?"

I was non-committal and mumbled, "Not really." In truth I was headed exactly to the spot they were pointing at on the screen. The spot with forecast snowfall of twelve inches. Not good, but somehow I wasn't surprised. I did some rapid calculations. A couple hours up, a couple more back, whatever time I spent there, and then I'd still need to get further south. I glanced at the TV again. It would be tight. The motel and some rest would have to wait. I had to get moving to beat the storm.

I looked in frustration at the television and mumbled, "Crud."

She got the meaning. "Well, you be careful. Those roads are treacherous enough when they're clear."

I looked her in the eye. "Thanks, I will." She flitted off to magically refill other unsuspecting patron's coffee cups.

Sated, I felt much better. Adding something besides stimulants to my diet had a remarkable effect. Even my hands were steady again. Ninja-waitress had dropped my bill off at some point. Nine bucks. Suddenly anxious to get underway, I didn't feel like waiting for change. I wanted to tip her well anyway. I dropped a twenty on the table and called it cheap.

I glanced once more at the TV. The storm was coming. The clock was ticking. It was time to for me to fly.

Sitting on the battered machine, adjusting my gloves and other gear, I was a bit surprised to see the waitress come out of the diner and approach my bike. She handed me a stainless steel thermos. Solid, tall and skinny, it's obvious quality was disguised by the "Freak's Diner" splayed across the side in obnoxiously loud colored letters. I looked up at the sign above the door, raised an eyebrow. The name wasn't even close.

She laughed at my expression. "A misprint. We've got a couple cases of 'em in before they fixed it. Normally we sell thermoses full of coffee to the truckers and road workers." She laughed again, "They even got the address wrong. We just give these away."

"Thank you. What's in it?" I turned and crammed it in the duffel on the back seat. My other delivery was in there. The thermos barely fit.

"Coffee, cream and sugar. Just how you made yours. Bring the thermos anytime you come…it's good for a free refill when you buy a meal." She patted me on the shoulder. "You be safe. Find shelter or get south before dark." She turned and headed back inside.

"I'll do my best." I said to her retreating back. I hoped it would be that easy.

***

There is little to compare with mountain riding, even when it's cold. Blue skies and bright sunlight helped to drive some of the chill away and insured the roads were clear of snow or ice…at least where there were no shadows.

Gently carving canyons, I pushed the big bike hard. I figured I had about five hours before the storm hit, and it was at least a couple hours to the target. I was a little fuzzy on exactly how much time it would take. I'd never run these roads in the winter. I leaned hard into the corners and let the heavy machine ply her trade. I began to grin as I felt my heart keeping time with the throbbing of the engine, my blood pumping with the rhythm of the road. Aches and pains faded as I flew into the wind. Man I love to ride!

I could stand a few hours of this, but all too soon it had to end.

The first oncoming car in miles, and it had to be a state police car. That shouldn't have been a problem. Even as hard as I was pushing, I wasn't really speeding. Not on these roads. The corners tended to have shadows, and the shadows tended to have snow or ice. In my rear-view mirror I saw brake lights. Great, it was going to be a problem. *Wonderful*.

It would take him a while to come around. There was no sense in making him chase me down. That'd just piss him off, and he'd catch up to me anyway. The road only went two directions, and my stop was near the middle. I found a safe place to pull out and shut her down. I was waiting there with my helmet off when he came flying around the corner, the low-profile LED light bar flashing his intentions.

He missed the stop, his keen sense of cop-trained observation only spotting the half-ton of black and chrome machine with the 300-pound guy standing beside it waiting for him AS he passed me by. He hit his brakes hard and chirped the tires as the anti-locks kicked in. I watched in amusement as he squealed right by. He turned around in the middle of the road, blocking both lanes as he burned rubber backing up and then taking off forward again. We were between blind corners and my eyes widened in disbelief. I'd have hated to come around one of those corners about now. This boded ill for the next few minutes. Unprofessional behavior in one aspect of their work usually predicts the same in the rest of it. He was as dangerous as could be in the car…and the car was the *least* dangerous thing this bozo had been issued. I mumbled to myself, "Yeah, tell me again that it's all about safety. Bloody friggen amateur."

Shortly I found myself locked in the back seat of the police cruiser. I wasn't handcuffed or under arrest, but had been put there for "my safety" as the man searched my bike. He wasn't following the rules, and since he's supposed to swear by them, by my book that clears me to not follow them also (if I was going to in the first place, they're not my rules). I had cooperated anyway. The formula was simple, he was armed and overly emotional and I wasn't either one at the moment. At least the cop car was warm.

I noted with amusement that his cruiser was equipped with video and it had a lovely view of the man playing games with my bike. That would help in case he broke anything…they'd at least know the reason if I had to toss his pompous, rights-violating, bullying ass right off the mountain.

At the moment he was trying to figure out how to release the seat. He was trying to get into my duffel bag on the back, and couldn't figure out the straps holding it. I had looped the main strap through the sissy bar, back through both of it's own handles, and then over the driver's backrest. Simple, secure, and easy to get on or off. Apparently he figured the backrest came off with the seat and he would have to do that to get the duffle loose. Sad, since even if he couldn't figure out that he needed to pull the one loop off the backrest, unclipping one of the ends of the long strap would also do the job. Any five year old would have had it off in seconds.

Releasing the seat takes the key, which was still in my pocket. I shook my head and chuckled. I figured I'd be here awhile but wasn't particularly worried about it. My only deadline was the oncoming storm, and I'd deal with it on my own terms. I lay back and closed my eyes. Some rest would do me good anyway.

The car rocking slightly started me awake. Instantly alert and clear-eyed, I glanced around. Maybe 45 minutes had passed. Another police car had arrived, and with some relief I noted that the second officer was much older. Chances were that now they could write me a ticket for whatever the hell they thought I'd done wrong, or not, and we could all get on with our lives. Life's too short to play these kinds of games. This particular mountain had taught me that, and it frustrated me a bit that they could live in the shadow of it and not know it.

Both men were leaning on the front of the car and discussing the contents of my duffle bag that were spread out on the hood. The younger cop was holding a small glass tube and gesturing, the older was examining the box he was pointing at.

I'd never seen the tube before, but I knew the box intimately. Anyone that had seen it would not soon forget it. Made of heavy oak, it measured a foot long by eight inches wide and four inches deep. The top was over an inch thick and ornately carved in very deep relief with two highly detailed dragons. The oak for the top was made from wood just off the heartwood of a very old oak. The very dark center color of the grain masterfully combined with the carving to render dark surface colors that got steadily lighter as the carving got deeper. The artist had used it to advantage, giving the dragons a startling three-dimensional effect. They fairly leapt off the cover of the box. Surrounded by clouds and lightning, they flew purposefully through the storm.

The top slid into a lip of the box itself and fit so tightly the seam was barely visible. I was honestly surprised the younger man had been able to open it without smashing it. He'd been struggling with just a duffle bag earlier.

The older man opened the box, looked inside, poked once at the contents with his finger, and then carefully replaced the lid. He glanced sharply at me before taking the glass vial from the other officer and then ushering him over to the far side of the other police car.

Returning, he opened the door, identified himself, and asked me to please step out of the car. At least he was polite.

I got out, stood up, and stretched luxuriously. "You guys done playing games yet? I've had about enough and I expect you know why."

He was watching me closely but didn't seem overly irritable. "Why didn't you tell him what was in the box?"

"He didn't ask."

"Fair enough. You could have told him when he asked to search the bike."

I looked him in the eyes, "It's none of his business. Yours either. Besides, he didn't ask that either. He also never identified himself or told me why he wanted to pull me over in the first place."

The man actually winced. He handed me my license. "You can collect your things and get on about your business, and I apologize. I'm his supervisor and I'll speak with him."

I said nothing but turned and carefully put the oak box and the rest of the contents back in the duffle bag. Placing it on the back seat of the Valkyrie I looked in disgust at the main strap. The man had actually had to cut it to get it off the bike. I unclipped the two ends and snarled as I tossed the ruined pieces on the hood of the police car. From one of my open side bags I grabbed a bungee cord and tied the duffle down with it instead. In short order I had everything stowed and the big machine ready to travel.

I started the engine and let it idle while I put on helmet and gloves. Finally ready to ride, I started to put the bike in gear, but paused as the older officer approached.

"Sir, I'm sorry, but here's the rest." He held out the glass vial I'd seen earlier.

I took it and held it up to the light to examine the contents. "Is that what I think it is?"

By way of an answer he held up the plastic wrapper it had come in, the label plainly visible. "Once again, I'm sorry sir. Anything I can do?"

I actually had some sympathy for the man. He seemed to be a professional that had been put in a difficult position by an incompetent subordinate. Still, a higher standard applies in this sort of case and if things really worked as they should, a subordinate with the attitude and lack of skills this one was exhibiting wouldn't have been allowed to be in a position to cause the problem in the first place. *Don't give guns to kids* and all that. The standards and oversight are falling every year. It's a sad thing when it has again become time in this country for the ordinary citizen to fear the police. Incompetence, malice, and a disregard for the very principles this country was founded on are becoming prevalent. They're still out there, and I salute them, but the professional, competent, and reasonable peace officer is becoming an endangered species.

I pointed at the video camera, "I'm formally requesting that the video be preserved." Let them stew on that for a while. "Also," I pointed at the other officer, "he owes me an apology, not you. He also owes me ten bucks for the strap."

I popped the bike into gear and roared up the mountain, scattering gravel and dust as I left the pullout.

* * *

I'd had to leave in a hurry just to maintain my dignity. I really didn't want to burst into laughter in front of them. The younger man needed a reprimand and the older one wouldn't take the situation seriously if he knew how I was feeling at the moment. The older officer had recognized the contents of the box immediately, as should anybody older then about six years old, but the other officer had not. I was finding that extremely funny at the moment, but then, I've always had a rather odd sense of humor.

Jack would have found it hilarious.

I laughed long and loud and then aggressively twisted the throttle on my machine. Heavy dark clouds were beginning to move in, and it was time for me to conclude this business. Pushing the bike to its limits, I grinned and leaned hard into the corners. I was speeding now. I doubted the cops would bother me again today, but I supposed they might. Either way, I was done making things easy for others for a while. They'd have to work at it if they tried.

Oh, the joke?

The vial was part of a field test kit and at the moment contained a clear liquid and a bit of the contents of the box. The box contained my next "delivery", which was several pounds of grayish powder, rather fine, but courser than say…powdered sugar. The grayish powder was ash.

The grayish powder was Jack…as in, his cremated remains.

He'd just been field tested to see if he was cocaine.

I feel so much better with these guys on the job.

***

A bleak mood descended on me even as the clouds covered the sun and turned the world to grey. It happened very fast. I shivered, and not just from the cold. A familiar landmark here, a haunting shadow on a turn in the road there, a landscape behind the trees. This was a familiar and foreboding place.

Shuddering, I grimly concentrated on my task, piloting the big motorcycle and carefully watching the road. I had to fight the urge to run...to point the powerful machine down the mountain and see how fast I could get off it...to see how fast I could get home. Feelings of loneliness nearly overwhelmed me, with hopelessness falling close behind. Half-seen things in my peripheral vision vanished when I turned to look. I stopped and removed my helmet, stabbing it on my backrest before moving on. It was making me claustrophobic, and I could feel things approaching that I couldn't see. The open and cold air didn't help much.

"Dammit Jack, why would you want to come *here*?" I yelled at the shadows, "Why bring *me*?" It was not the first time I had asked those questions. There were no answers...at least none that I could hear.

Spirits and demons were wandering this place.

Close...I was getting very close.

Part 5—Monuments to the Dead

I realized before I rounded the corner that this was the place. The tension and unease on the air reached a pinnacle and right on queue the turn-off for the scenic overlook slid into view. I pulled slowly into the narrow parking lot. The place hadn't changed much and I wasn't sure why I had expected it to. The parking lot was a little bigger, the guardrail was much heavier, and a larger deck had been added, but the mountain was the same. The view hadn't changed and that just didn't seem right. The world sure had.

I ran the big bike right to the narrowest end of the empty lot. A pair of portable johns took up the end parking place so I pulled the Valkyrie up on the sidewalk behind them and shut her down. She would not be visible from the road or parking lot on casual inspection. In the face of the approaching weather I wasn't expecting anybody to stop here, but it was worth the precaution. I didn't want to be disturbed.

An eerie silence swept in at the loss of the engine noise. The back of my neck tingled. Dismounting I quickly turned, ready to confront what I was sure was sneaking up on me, but there was nothing there. I shivered inside my heavy leather jacket, and not from the cold. The atmosphere was oppressive, and I could almost taste it. My shoulders and arms ached from the tension. I closed my eyes and, breathing deeply, forced myself to relax muscle by muscle.

Shortly I detected a new smell on the air. Cold, earthy, damp, and a bit smoky, it heralded more problems to come. Snow was falling somewhere. I opened my eyes even as I felt the first flakes graze my face. The ride down was going to get interesting. Even now the winds were whipping up and the visibility was dropping rapidly.

I grabbed the heavy duffel off my back seat and immediately regretted the loss of the long strap to throw over my shoulder. I'm could've rigged something up, but didn't want to take the time. The spirits of this place were tangible and I couldn't stay in one place for long. I kept turning to see what was coming and there was never anything there but snow. I shrugged and grabbed the duffle by the handles. I didn't have all that far to go anyway.

Searching near the end of the guardrail for the small trail I knew was there, I quickly located it and started down. I was carefully noting landmarks as I went, the parking area was difficult to see from below and the trail would rapidly become obscured as the snow accumulated.

A hundred feet along and a switchback later the trail widened and there was a small granite monument beside it. About a foot square at the base; it tapered to a point at about five feet tall. A tall, skinny pyramid. Etched letters in vertical line from thin top to about half way down read, "In memory of". The list of names was in smaller, horizontal script below that.

Monuments to the dead. I despise them. We build far, far too many of them, and I'm not sure why. The living are left to muddle through as best they can...the survivors ignored...shunned even...but the dead we carve in stone so we remember. I remembered, despite my best efforts to forget. I didn't need the damn stone.

This monument, like so many around the country, celebrated not the dead, but rather, it commemorated what killed them. A stark reminder. A victory dance. A tribute to the act itself, not the result. I tasted blood and realized I'd clamped my jaw tightly shut. Once again I tried in vain to relax.

I didn't need to read the names, I'd been trying to forget them for more than two decades and they were still indelibly etched in my memory. I knew what would be inscribed there, but I was inexorably drawn look anyway. Snow was beginning to collect and obscure the names, but I could still make out how many there were. I quickly smashed down a flash of anger. There were enough violent emotions in the air here. Still, I was dismayed. There was one too many names carved into the stone.

Flushing, I stepped forward and brushed the snow off. I was right...sort of. There had been an extra name, inscribed as the others were, but it had later been crudely gouged out of the stone, leaving a ragged and ugly line in its place. That was interesting. Reading the remaining names, I grunted in satisfaction and moved on. The correct one had been obliterated. Apparently at least one other person still knew the truth of this place.

I walked through two more switchbacks. Several hundred feet down the trail and perhaps 60 feet in elevation below the parking area the trail widened and flattened to a large granite outcropping. This was the place. Sheltered by a slight overhang above, a rock wall to one side, and the steep trail to the other, there was little wind here. That was helpful. I could hear it in the distance whipping through the trees producing a steady roar. The white noise was occasionally punctuated by a long, whistling moan and I found it extremely unnerving.

I moved to the far end of the rocky area, right where the trail switched back again and continued down into the valley. Just off the trail and against the rock wall a flat stone outcropping formed a slight overhanging platform. This would do.

I brushed the light dusting of snow off the rock and looked out into the valley as it swirled away in the winds. Everything nearby was beginning to turn white, and the blowing heavy snow obscured anything further away. I looked up. This storm was going to get dangerous. It would be dark soon too.

I knelt and opened the duffel. I was surprised at how warm the dragon box was as I pulled it out. I ran my hands over the wood. It was truly a masterwork of rare design. I could almost feel the two carved dragons moving under my fingers. There was power here, and I was finally ready to admit that, even if I wasn't sure I understood. I looked carefully at the lid, absorbing every detail of the dragons flying purposefully through the storm. I then closed my eyes, covered them with my hands, and felt them as they came to life…

***

The great dragon soars, alone, flying and free. Simple joy found twisting on the winds, moving where it wills, blown only by a whim.

Sometime later he detects a patterns to the winds; subtle pressures pushing this way and that. Curious, the dragon follows; twisting just so, tasting the air…carried by intangible guides to an unknown end. Who is calling him? To where? Why?

A place is reached. The pressures vanish. The guide is gone. Expectation hangs on the air and taints the winds. Suddenly the dragon knows it is not alone. Another has been brought here as well. And there is something else…

Jack and I never met before that day. Indeed we came from completely different directions, some quirk of the universe bringing us to that particular place at that exact time. Jack arrived from the west on his 500cc dual-sport at the same moment I slowly climbed the road from the east on my struggling little street 125cc. We were both just young bucks wandering...finding a few days off from work, scraping up a couple extra dollars for gas, and picking destinations on a whim. We both tended to wander often and far.

Two dragons together. Two of one mind, two of common blood. There is no time to celebrate. There is scarcely time to understand. Turning as one, the dragons sense a new presence. Old and crafty. Powerful, fast, and unfettered. Unleashed? Indefinable. Beyond comprehension.

The dragons stir uneasily. The new presence is not a dragon. And it's hungry...

Hours later, beaten and bloodied, our bodies and spirits numb and abused, we left the mountain riding together. Unspoken agreements had passed between us. We were both proud men that had endured more than we should, and now we wanted nothing more complicated than just to get home. We knew we'd need each other's help. Besides, we wouldn't admit it, but at the moment neither of us could stand to be alone. We looked into a place no man should see, and we knew what could be waiting out there. It would be a long time before either of us came to terms with that.

The dragons' fates were linked, and they knew it.

A gas stop in New Mexico had produced the box. Souvenirs were the last things on our mind, but while waiting in line to pay for our fuel, we had spotted it among some Native American merchandise on a small table. Jack and I had both reached for it at the same time. We both felt the energy when we touched it. The old man running the place had laughed.

"Two dragons," he pointed at the box, then at us, "for two dragons." That was when we discovered we both carried the same nickname, "Dragon".

He gave it to us, somehow understanding there was no way we could pay for it. "It's yours, and only yours," he told us, "it holds your spirits," his eyes had grown sad, "You must set them free."

We hadn't understood what he meant, but we had the box. It seemed a small victory, but we needed small victories then.

The box had gone home with Jack, simply because his bike could carry more. It wasn't something either of us required possession of, but rather, it seemed enough that we each knew it was safe.

***

The intricately carved dragons grew even warmer, nearly alive, and I decided it was time. Opening my eyes, I pulled the lid off and carefully dumped Jack's ashes in a pile on the rock, glancing at and then corralling the newspaper clipping that had been in the bottom of the box. Reaching in the duffel, I pulled the several small sticks of oak I had carried along with the box, breaking the smaller ones as I put them in a stacked square pattern on top of the ashes. I wadded the clipping up and carefully placed it in the middle of the kindling. The box bottom followed, and then I propped the lid against it so I could see the dragons.

I pulled a lighter from my pocket and in one smooth motion, reached over and lit the paper. I could see the headline as the burning clipping uncurled and turned brown, "Eight Killed in Accident."

They'd had it wrong of course, but history often records only what people want to believe. The truth is seldom relevant.

I pulled the thermos full of coffee out and discarded the empty duffel to the side. Silently thanking the thoughtful waitress, I poured myself a cup of the hot creamy colored liquid and sipped at it. I sat with my back against the wall just a few feet from the growing fire. I watched the flames lick around the box and did my best to relax. It would be a little while. I had enough wood for a respectable fire there.

Slowly the fire grew, the dry oak crackling. The wind noise faded from the background and the heat bouncing off the rocks began to warm me. Fascinated, I stared at the dragons. They stared back, fighting their way though the storm, flying in the flames. They seemed right at home there.

***

I could hear the yelling even over my engine as I pulled into the parking lot. I was a latecomer to the scene, but not by much. Smoke and dust still billowed from where the car had accelerated from a standing stop, smashed through the railing, and plummeted over the edge.

I jumped off the bike, peered over the edge. *Oh jheeze...* Out loud I muttered, "Holy crap!"

I was vaguely aware of another bike sliding to a stop behind me.

One lady stood next to a car, several kids were in the back seat. She was wringing her hands. Yeah, that'll help. I turned to her, "Is this your car?"

There was no response. She was starting to cry. I grabbed her by the shoulders, turned her away from the scene and yelled, "IS THIS YOUR CAR!"

She seemed to see me for the first time. "Yes..."

I propelled her toward the door, pulled it open. "Go! Get some help. Find a phone. Cops! Ambulance! Something!" She didn't move. I swatted her hard on the rump. "HURRY!" Relieved to be told what to do, she nodded and quickly got in her car. She was backing out even as I turned toward the trail.

***

I opened my eyes to falling darkness and the echoes of screams fading on the wind. I was startled; I hadn't realized I'd slipped into sleep. I wouldn't have thought that possible here. Snow was falling even heavier now, imparting a hushed sound upon the world despite the wind noise. Blinking, I poured more coffee. The fire had grown, but the box hadn't really caught yet.

"Dammit Jack..." I hadn't wanted to relive this, but it seemed that I must. I stared into the fire, wondering. Was Jack the lucky one here?

***

Disruption in the patterns, a bad taste on the winds. The dragons saw it then, this thing of dark light. Saw it. Felt it. Feared it.

Two died in the car. I would later believe they probably died above rather than on impact, but by that time nobody cared.

Two dead. Blood running across the stone. So much blood, the tangy, metallic smell of it so strong I could taste it. Intense desire to help, but knowing it was already too late for them. Others were hurt too. There had been people on the trail, maybe others in the car. Passersby wanting to help. Chaos reigned.

Human nature makes us slow to recognize danger. We want to believe the best. The enemy here was the car wreck, and it was finished. Wasn't it?

The dragons watched the dark light seek out a wind, a motion, a life. Touch it. Surround it. Consume it. They weren't sure what they were seeing. Finished, the entity looked at the dragons then. Dismissed them with disdain. Turned away and touched another wind. It screamed and was consumed almost instantly.

Two more died while we watched. We were just kids. We didn't understand.

The dark light moved on to another wind. Another life. Touched it…surrounded it…

Another died even as we struggled to believe. We'd failed her…and I can still see her eyes.

***

"We were just kids!"

I opened my eyes again, tears streaming down my cheeks and the echoes of my scream…my apology…my pain…reverberating across the valley.

I listened to the echoes die. *Please. No more.* Nauseous, I snarled, "Fuck this!" and unsteadily lurched to my feet. Struggling not to retch I turned and stumbled up the trail.

I didn't make it far. The malevolence in the valley was like a wall of brambles. The harder I pushed through it the harder it got to move and the more it hurt. I stopped and stood swaying on my feet, fists clenched, my back to the fire. I turned slowly, till I faced it again, the tears still falling.

A deep breath, a quiet voice, "God Jack. Why'd you bring me here?"

The crackling fire was my only answer.

Part 6—Soaring

Slowly, unwillingly, I made my way back to the fire, slumped down, and leaned against the wall. The snow was really coming down now. I poured more coffee and sighed. *The hell with it.* I've endured a lot throughout my life. I could stand a little more. Jack wanted to come here. I had to bring him. There really wasn't any choice.

The fire was fully involved now, burning cheerily in defiance of the feelings in this place. I stared into the flames. The dragons were free of the box lid now, the thinner wood burning away before the heavy figures. I watched them, my eyes half-lidded. Soon, they began to move within the flames.

***

The dragons roared in rage and disbelief. What was this thing? What was it doing? Why was it here?

I cried out at what I'd seen. There was an echoing, strangled exclamation beside me.

I turned my head; saw Jack for the first time.

The man totally ignored us, moved toward the next person, an injured man, scrambling, crawling to get away.

Jack looked at me. Our eyes met. Fear, understanding, the beginnings of comprehension, an unspoken agreement.

The instinct is to run. It is not a minor thing. A man will not.

We weren't men, at least according to society, but we were on the verge. Teenagers shouldn't have to try to understand things like this.

We didn't understand, but we had to act. Nodding in unison, we rushed the scene. The fight was on!

A man with a knife is not so big a threat…not really a problem to deal with, as long as you're not afraid of the knife. To focus on it gives it power. Always watch the man, not the weapon. The weapon's not doing the killing. That was our first lesson. We learned it quickly.

Two dragons move as one. Sinuous, fast, and powerful, they charge the dark light. The old power calmly watches them come and repels them easily, casually. They aren't the only things that are fast. They aren't the most powerful. Stunned, they gather themselves and charge again.

The man was unnaturally strong. He'd thrown us clear and recovered before we realized what had happened. His back was to me as he charged Jack with the knife. As I got to my feet, almost magically my hands held a head-sized rock. I had no idea where it came from.

He had to be stopped. There was no question. But even then I hadn't really acknowledged the peril of the situation. Even then I didn't comprehend.

We've been indoctrinated all our lives to be civil, not to lash out, to suppress the rage, the fight, the strength. Taught to hold back the dark side of the man. Schooled to be sensitive, understanding, calm. Taught that violence is never necessary—it's always wrong. I stepped in; he was exposed. I could have brought the rock down on his head. Despite what I'd seen, I hesitated, made a choice. I brought it down on his arm instead.

With an audible crack his arm broke. The knife went flying. The rock tumbled out of my grip. Scarcely hesitating the man turned and swept me off my feet, landing a kick to my stomach. The breath swooshed out of me and colors swam before my vision.

Trying to get to my feet, I realized I wasn't going to make it. The man was already reaching for me. I rolled away, tried again, but he was fast, pressing his advantage.

Behind him, Jack had a bat sized stick, raised it to swing. Somehow the man knew he was there, turned. I didn't expect it to matter. He wasn't going to make it, I was sure Jack had he upper hand. Even then the stick was on its way toward the man's head. We had him!

The man completed his turn and faced Jack.

Jack froze in mid-swing, a strange look on his face. I screamed, "Don't stop! Get him!" but it was too late. The man made a move I didn't quite follow and just like that, Jack was gone, swept over the edge of the rocks.

I had regained my feet and somehow found another rock in my hands. This time I would do what was needed. This time I wouldn't hesitate. This time I…

He spun to face me, our eyes met…

The dragon finally has the advantage and presses in. He knows without a doubt that he can finish it. Muscles flex, sinews tense. A graceful move, a step, readying the final blow. The thing of darkness and light spins to face him. Their eyes meet. The dragon sees the seething chaos in the entity, and for the first time, beholds its soul…

Uh oh…

Without so much as a sound, a rock falls slowly to the ground.

I was sliding down the steep slope with nary a clue as to how I got here. In reflex I spread arms and legs wide to stop the tumbling and slow down. Ignoring abrasions and pain, I grabbed for rocks and sticks and clawed at the dirt trying to stop the slide. I was too stunned to cry out.

Suddenly my outstretched hand met flesh. He caught my arm, first try, a solid wrist-to-wrist grip. I was jerked up short, white-hot pain seizing my shoulder. The pull flipped me over. We both slid a few feet more but Jack had braced himself well. I rolled to my knees but still he held on. I looked up, our eyes met. I could read it there. *Behind you…*

Turning my head I gasped. Mere inches past my feet the steep slope ended abruptly. There was at least a 40-foot sheer drop to the rugged landscape below. I braced myself firmly and nodded. He carefully released his grip when he was sure I was steady. Our eyes met again. The job wasn't done and we both knew it. I had failed, even as Jack had before me. No words were needed.

Adrenalin is a powerful thing. It only took us a moment to scramble up the steep slope, but that was about a half-a-moment too long. Even as we crested the slope another one died. We both heard the strangled cry of pain and terror. With a sinking heart we knew we'd failed him too.

Two dragons, moving as one. Steely resolve. They'd failed before. There would not be a next time…there were more winds about. More lives. The stakes were unthinkably high. The cost of failure was much too great.

The fight was on again. Motions too fast to follow. The knife was back, then gone again. I took another solid hit but kept on my feet. Jack went flying but landed on his. I ducked to the back, Jack crossed to the front. We somehow knew what the other was going to do, where the other was going to move. It gave us an edge.

It almost wasn't enough.

Power converged, strength combined. The dragons surround and engulf the entity. Bodies writhe. Fight. Light streams into the darkness. The darkness soaks it up, unfazed.

Even with the broken arm, the man was still horribly strong. Jack and I were tiring fast but the man kept fighting. We didn't realize it, but he was guiding the fight. Very slowly, we drew closer and closer to the slope. Had we been older...more experienced, we might have caught on.

I was surprised when I stepped off the edge. Jack was too. Too late, we saw the ploy.

Dismayed, the dragons merge once more. A last attempt, a desperate try, a futile motion. We must not fail again! The light strengthens, flashes. Success!

Falling, I made a last frantic grab. My hand connected, gripped. I barely had the man by the cuff of his jeans. Jack had him by the back pocket.

Apart we couldn't have done it. Neither grip was enough alone but together they spun him around and off his feet. All three of us tumbled over the edge and slid down the steep slope. Grappling, entangled, there was no reaching out to slow the fall, no stopping the slide. Rapidly we approached the cliff.

Falling, tumbling, tossed by the currents and the winds, the dragons plummet. They push apart, release the enemy. One grabs the other, the other grabs the one. One goes over the cliff, the other screams in defiance and tightens his grip. Muscles bulge, joints pop, sinew tears. Flesh ripped on the rocks. Pain flashes through their souls.

But they don't fall.

One saved the other. Neither was ever sure which.

The enemy flies into the abyss, smashes on the rocks below. The dark light explodes and fades away, its passing leaving an ugly color to the winds. Just like that, it is done. The fight is over. The threat is ended.

The dragons have no strength to celebrate though. It's all they can do simply to breathe.

***

My eyes wide open now, I stared into the remains of the fire. A small pile of ash and embers smoldered, occasionally emitting a spark, while a thin streak of smoke rises a few feet before vanishing in the winds.

I grimly recalled the statistics. Eight people died on the mountain that day. Seven of the names were on the monument at the trailhead. The eighth had been rightfully obliterated. There were five survivors, not including Jack and me. There were six other witnesses of various parts of the event, including the woman and her kids that had gone for help. The police asked questions, never quite understanding what happened. We didn't lie, we just weren't exactly sure to begin with, and they never asked quite the right questions.

They tabulated all the statements and information, and when the story came out in the paper, it was of a tragic accident. The official story was that the driver hit the gas instead of the brake, bearing the two in the car and four other victims off the upper sidewalk to the crash site some sixty feet below. Two hikers on the trail at the crash site were also killed.

They weren't stupid. They just wanted to believe. We weren't stupid either. We let them. It was, after all, the sane explanation.

Sane can be good.

I stood slowly and brushed the snow off myself. I had some thinking to do. Reliving this event now, when I had so much more life experience, had given me a slightly different outlook on it. I'd always felt that we had failed, and people had died. Maybe that wasn't true. We had done what we could, and people had lived.

For years I'd tried to make sense of things. Even now I still wonder...*why?* But standing by the fire I finally realized something. The truth of it is, there is no answer. There *can be* no answer. There is no situation, no reason, no excuse that could drive somebody to do...to *become* what we saw. It cannot be justified or understood. It simply will not fit in the human framework.

I'd never forget, but maybe now it would be okay for me to remember. Maybe now I could heal.

I pulled Jack's note out of my pocket. His personal requests to me.

Item one was the delivery. It was done.

Item two concerned the will and dispensation of the funds. I had taken care of that as soon as I read his intentions. His note said, *"Daniel, I love my wife, and believe she should have it all. It's your call. Speak a word and it will be arranged as I wish. Or take it all for yourself. You might have a choice. I doubt it, but I had to be sure."*

I hadn't even thought about it. *"Arrange it."*

Standing here, I finally understood why Jack had done it that way. *The smell of sex in the room. The redhead that had been mine. Jack and Karen together in my bed.* He had found his happiness, and somewhere deep down he wondered if he had betrayed me in doing so...questioned if he had taken mine. He wondered if he *owed* me, and had given me the way to exact payment. I think he knew the answer, but still felt bound to ask the question. If I regret anything of this, it's that we had been apart so long that he felt the need to wonder. Life. It's complicated that way.

The third request was cryptic. Only I would have understood it. *"It holds more than it contains. Set us free."* He was talking about the box. *"As for me, well, I want the same thing you do. I want to soar where I fell. I want to fly where I failed."*

I dropped the note in the fire, watched it catch and burn to ash.

I closed my eyes, deeply inhaled the cold air.

"What spirits haunt you here, Dragon?" It was Jack's voice.

I opened my eyes, smiled. Now, after all these years, I knew the answer.

I spoke it aloud, "Only those I carry with me."

Already the oppression of the valley had lifted. The darkness shadowing my every move vanished as if it never was.

In a smooth motion I stepped forward and with the side of my boot, swept the small pile of ash and embers off the stone and over the drop.

"Fly…"

They caught in a rushing updraft and the embers burst into life. Small flames mixed with the snowflakes, tossed and swirled into the night sky in a dazzling display of light and motion; an unfettered dance of transition, joy, and ecstasy.

A spirit released. A dragon born.

I watched for a moment, and then, my spirit soaring and tears clouding my eyes, turned my back on the overwhelming display of power and emotion.

I quietly whispered, "Goodbye Jack," and without looking back I walked briskly up the trail.

Epilog

It took six hours to get off the mountain alone. Deep snow is easier to ride in than slush and ice, but I still had to keep the speeds way down. By the time I came off the mountain the bike and I were covered in ice. The heat from the engine would melt the snow a bit and it would refreeze anywhere it stuck. My jeans were frozen to my boots, and I'd had to stop several times to kick accumulations of ice off the wheels and suspension.

It was still a bit early for breakfast as I rolled past the diner, but they were getting ready. The lights were on and people were moving around inside. I turned around. Half frozen and covered in ice I banged on the front door.

My waitress from the day before unlocked the door and peeked out, "Wha…?"

I held up the thermos. "You said anytime…" My hands were shaking.

"God honey, you look horrible."

"Thank you," I smiled.

"Where've you been?"

I smiled even more; a small town waitress ought to know better than asking that question; there'd be no telling what she'd hear. I laughed a bit, "Oh, you know…cops, mountains, blizzards, ghosts, dragons…the usual stuff," I shook the thermos a bit, "Can I con you out of some coffee?"

She grabbed my hand and pulled me inside. "Not unless I fix you some breakfast," she paused, halfway to seating me at a table, "You WILL be heading south now?"

It was not *quite* a question. You gotta love small towns.

***

I parked the bike in front of the small office building and stumbled inside. The secretary ushered me right in to the inner, private office.

The lawyer was there. He had a talent for always appearing to have been waiting, just for me. That's a good thing. "Yes?"

"It's done."

He smiled, "Thank you. But I've no idea what you're talking about. By the way, Karen would like to see you."

I narrowed my eyes, "Briefly I hope?"

He had her there inside of ten minutes. The secretary ushered Karen into the office and then the lawyer left us alone.

Karen stood there like an embarrassed schoolgirl, hands clasped and rocking on her feet a bit.

I prompted her, "Yes?"

"He told me," she waved her hands toward the outer office, "what you did...that you signed over the estate to me."

"Yes."

"Why?"

"Jack asked me to."

"But after what...well..." she wrung her hands and stomped a little in frustration, "Why? You could have kept it. You must have been tempted?"

I said nothing. She still didn't understand and I expected, never would.

Finally she smiled a bit. She was so much prettier when she smiled. "Well, thank you Daniel." She smiled even prettier, straightened up a bit.

I could have her now if I wanted to. She could be mine again. Her body language was clear. Despite her new riches, she needed someone in her life. Someone to hold, someone to make her feel needed, someone she held power over. She thought she knew where she stood with me.

I stood and walked to the door.

She stepped forward, extending her arm, "It must have been a tough choice."

Ignoring the arm and opening the door, I looked over my shoulder at her. Tough choice? No. There had never been any choice at all.

"Goodbye Karen."

***

I arrived home just barely in time to greet the wife, returning from her own trip. I had managed to shower and change clothes, but hadn't had any food or sleep yet. I'd been out of the ice and snow for many hundreds of miles now, but ice was still melting and shluffing off the bike in the garage.

She got her first good look at me, "God honey, you look horrible."

This time I laughed, "Thank you."

"What happened? Where've you been?"

I laughed even more; my wife ought to know better than asking me that. Grinning I said, "Oh, you know…cops, mountains, blizzards, ghosts, dragons…the usual stuff,"

She looked at me sternly, her eyes betraying the laughter behind them, "Really…."

She gets the truth from me, always, but sometimes there is no simple answer.

I started to talk, stopped, thought a moment, sighed. "There was something I had to do…"

She stopped me with a hug and kiss. When she was done she said, laughing, "I know, I know…sometimes you've just gotta ride." She spun me towards the bed. "Get some sleep. I'll have dinner ready in a while."

Sometimes you've just gotta ride.

Yeah…yeah I do.

I turned to the bed, but never remembered getting in it. As I lay there something occurred to me.

I've been asked of my nickname, "Do you dream you're a dragon?"

I thought about Jack, about the experience of riding, about my life, about the magic in the world, and about that night on the mountain.

The room faded away, mists and stars surrounding me, embers flying into a storm.

Maybe I am a man, only dreaming that I'm a dragon.

But perhaps I am a dragon, only dreaming that I'm a man.

***

Drifting high on the swirling currents, I felt the chest muscles rippling as sweeping wings carried me aloft. Blood pumping through massive arteries bore oxygen gleaned from the rarified air by powerful lungs. A furnace...an engine of infinite power and complexity, a man, a mount, and strangely something much more than all, the Dragon soared effortlessly through the night.

Minor alterations, muscles tensed, sinews relaxed. A glance, subtle movements...and the flight changed. Almost randomly or at a whim, entire worlds slide by. Realities distort as the beast plummets nearly to its destruction, only to scream in joyous ecstasy and climb back to the heights—simply to do it all over again.   It is chaos unleashed to any observing, but actually tightly, precisely controlled— a dance of intricate design, influenced only by the dancers, the flowing passion, and the stars above.

And then there's the music...

Polar Bear Ride

Why do we do the things we do? Sometimes the answer is complicated, rooted deep and dark inside our souls.
Then again, sometimes it's not.

I'm sure you've read of those wackos that go swimming in ice water in January somewhere up north...we have something similar here in Texas...except by "we" I mean "I". Um...and no offence to the whackos if you are one. I'm sure those long months of cold and darkness do strange things to the mind...heh heh...

Well, it's kind of tradition...January first of each year, regardless of the weather, I go for a ride. I dunno how it started, but my current theory is that it was something myself and my roommate (Hi James! I'm pretty sure this is your fault!) came up with about 25 years ago...on a January first...and I expect, directly after consuming a rather large amount of alcohol (anti-freeze) in celebration of the new year.

Over the years, the alcohol consumption has markedly tapered off...but the stupid tradition somehow hasn't managed to. Ya know, tradition. Ah well, if you gotta have traditions, they may as well involve riding...or sex...or...rather...riding AND sex...hmmm...

But I digress.

Anyway, on New Year's day I've ridden in temperatures as low as six degrees, and several times in the ice, but in the case of the ice, it's usually only to the end of the driveway and back. I did make 25 miles in a snowstorm once...and that was basically to see what kind of expressions I could find on folks faces in town. It was almost worth it, and at least the cops were nice about the whole thing.

Once I had to...ur...acquire a bike to ride on January 1. I was between machines at the moment. Test rode a Harley that year, I did. They thought I was nuts too (it was 24 degrees and sleeting), but at least the cops were nice about the whole thing. I'd have bought the damn thing too, except I didn't have enough money left for the down payment after I made bail. So much for great customer service.

So...as to today's Polar bear ride. Well, 74 degrees and balmy. Couple hundred miles in the breezy Texas winter. I got sunburned. Found about 70 other machines to meet for lunch (Hey to the Southern Cruisers and Texas VRCC).

Riding on January first...in my shirtsleeves. Jeans and a t-shirt. January first...

Gotta love those Texas winters.

Ahhhh...

Steel Wheels

Life and living are simply not the same thing. They aren't even close.

I listen to the hissing, howling sound of steel wheels on steel track and watch the seated people sway in unison with the not-so-gentle sideways rocking of the transit train. All of them, like me, sit in silence and wait for their stop. All of them hope for the end of their journey. Some of them read or listen to headsets to pass the time, but all of them, when I can see their faces, have the same look in their eyes. There is no enjoyment here. They, like me, have been reduced to simple endurance.

This is no way to travel.

Shortly the depressing atmosphere becomes too much and I turn my head to look out at dingy predawn light through the rain streaked window. It helps some, as I can at least dream.

Flying, free, alive...

***

I've been told a man should know his limits. Or, at very least, a man should know the limits of those around him. This morning dawned cold and wet, with constant heavy rain flooding the streets and reducing visibility. The TV reported no end in sight, and also began reporting dire traffic conditions caused by accidents and standing water on the roads.

I glanced at the big Valkyrie cruiser in the garage and sighed. She is certainly capable of handling such conditions, as am I. We have cheerfully ridden in much worse, but today was not to be. I simply needed to commute into work and didn't feel like dodging the errant cars and incompetent drivers that were already clogging the freeways. I was more worried about one of them not coping properly with the conditions and taking me out, than I was of running into something I couldn't handle on my own. My wife had been looking a bit strained anyway as I reached for my leather jacket. She never says anything, but I know she worries nonetheless. *A man should know his limits.* I hung the jacket back up. Today I would take the train.

I hopped in my *Big Iron*, my truck, and breathed a sigh of relief that she actually started. I noted that the inspection sticker had expired three months ago and promised myself that I would drive her more often. I guess I'm supposed to start those cage thingies every once and a while. A quick trip to the train station, and a half-mile slog through the rain brought me to the southbound platform, drenched despite my umbrella.

***

Nearly an hour later I was still leaning my head against the cool glass, listening to the hissing of the wheels and staring longingly out the window at the cold, wet world. I had lost my annoyance at the water leaking around the seal and dripping on my legs and was just hoping desperately for this ride to end. Funny, had I been on the motorcycle, I would have arrived twenty minutes earlier and been disappointed that it had ended so quickly. Odd, how experience colors the world.

At my stop, I had to cross the tracks to head toward my destination, and I stopped on the northbound platform. It took me fully five minutes to suppress the irrational and nearly overwhelming urge to catch the next north-bounder and go back and get my bike. Resolve set in and I decided that in the future nothing short of an ice storm would keep me from riding when I was in the mood.

Yes, a man should know his limits. I guess I just found one of mine.

I listen to the hissing, howling sound of steel wheels on steel track and watch the seated people. All of them, when I can see their faces, have the same look in their eyes. There is no enjoyment here. They, like me, have been reduced to simple endurance.

Simple endurance. Yah. This is no way to travel.

Life is a road…

The Wet Driveway Principle

There are no absolutes. Heh heh.

Weather in Texas is an interesting thing. Yeah, I know we talk about it too much, but what the hell else are we going to talk about in a world where many people are so determined to be offended by something that even the mention of the word "Christmas" sends them into a foaming at the mouth frenzy? (and of course their counterparts are severely offended by the phrase "Happy Holidays" to a ridiculous level).

I mean, what the heck am I supposed to say? "Merry New Thanksmas Chrisyear?"

Oh, and as an aside: Merry Christmas AND Happy Holidays! Offended? Well, you're working too hard at it. Get over it. Life's so much bigger than that.

Anyway, I digress, as usual.

Where was I? Oh yes, the weather. Well, that and motorcycles of course. Who do you think you're talking to here?

I'll ride in any conditions...it's required in order to do any kind of serious miles, but that said, I'll tend to avoid commuting to work on the bike if it's raining cats and dogs outside. After all, bugs in my teeth are bad enough...picking dogs and cats out takes some serious flossing. Heck, just last week I took *Big Iron* to work instead of the bike...the 19 degrees and 20 full miles of black ice between me and the job being the main factor in that decision. Even the trains were screwed that day.

The problem is, here in Texas anyway; you cannot depend on the weather forecasts. There are two groups of people trying to issue them—weathermen and meteorologists.

"Weatherman" apparently means they have a dartboard with various predictions on it and they are not very good at darts. THOCK! "Hey, I hit the corner of the board! That's marked 'scattered showers'. Better issue a tornado warning!"

"Meteorologist" means they couldn't afford the dartboard after paying for that degree, but they are actually slightly better at predictions because they DO still have the darts and also merit a window in their office. SMASH! TINKLE! "Hey! My dart went out the window! OMG! What the HELL is that? Is that a cloud? It is! It is! A cloud! Agggghhh! Issue a winter storm warning! Buy batteries! Boil some water! Hide the children!"

Have I digressed again?

Back to the point. If I didn't ride when they predicted nasty weather...I'd never get to ride.

So, all this leads to, 'The Wet Driveway Principle'. I came up with that many years ago to describe my decisions regarding the weather when I start out on a trip or commute.

Basically, if the driveway is NOT wet, I ride. I completely ignore the forecasts, except strictly as entertainment value.

Then there's this morning. It rained...at least I guess I can call it that. The driveway was wet anyway.

I stepped out into the warm balmy air and stared up at the full moon peeking through the clouds. It seemed to me that this event was over, but the weather guys had been too busy gleefully predicting sleet and snow for next weekend to bother to talk about NOW.

Hmmm. 'The Wet Driveway Principle' should apply. The driveway was, after all, wet. That little smidgeon of rain would bring out the worst on the highway too. Oil and diesel fuel would rise to the top but not wash off. Basically as bad as it gets without the roads actually being covered in ice...or fire. We had some of both last week, but that would be another story.

I inhaled deeply of the early morning air. Balmy nights in December. Gotta love those Texas winters. My hands were shaking and deep within my soul the passion stirred. I fired up the mp3 player—twelve hours of my favorite music in essentially random order—just to see what it selected.

Time for Me to Fly by REO Speedwagon was its most appropriate selection.

I glared at the player. I'm thinking the thing is just plain evil. My throttle hand was twitching.

I looked again at the wet driveway and grumbled softly to myself, "The hell with it." I hopped on the bike and headed downtown at what was no doubt an unsafe speed. The lonely wail of the big Valkyrie's engine echoed off the concrete walls of the deserted freeways as the moon raced me through the cityscape.

As for 'The Wet Driveway Principle'? Well, for today anyway, it'll have to be the 'Kind-of Wet Driveway Principle', or maybe the 'Almost Not Wet Driveway Principle'.

Whatever. As long as I get to ride.

I'll see you on the (almost not wet) road.

City of Mist

The ride.

I've often said that there is no such thing as four o'clock in the morning. Oh our theories and time measuring devices insist that it actually exists, but it has never really been sited by anything resembling a reliable witness. I mean, who's going to believe somebody that gets up that early anyway?

I grabbed the keys off the dresser and reflexively stuffed my cell phone in my back pocket. I didn't bother to turn it on. I'm not even sure why I carry it. The perverse nature of the universe absolutely guarantees that it never works when I might need it for something and there was no chance I would be answering it this morning. The only reason I even possess the thing is that my job occasionally requires it.

Despite my efforts to not disturb my wife her sleepy voice asked, "Hmm? Where are you going?"

I smiled in the dark, moved to the bedside, and gently kissed her on the neck. She was lying on her side with her back to me and my mood and expression turned serious. I pondered the world and the passions that move me as I gently ran a finger up her thigh and over the curve of her hip. I slid onto the bed behind her and fluidly continued the stroking motion into a hug that culminated with our bodies pressed together and my right hand cupping her breast. She was delightfully warm. I gave her another kiss, this time on the ear. She gave a gentle shiver and a quiet moan. In the subdued light coming from the hall I could see she was smiling.

I whispered into her ear, "Going riding babe." I released her, rolled off the bed, and pulled the covers up over her shoulders.

As I was leaving the room she contentedly mumbled, "Be safe." and instantly succumbed to sleep.

I had told her the truth…I always do…but the answer was pretty much irrelevant. I could have said anything at all. Mundane or completely outrageous, she wouldn't remember it anyway. Predawn on a Sunday morning will do that to her. When she wakes up at a more reasonable hour she will remember that I had an errand to attend to at work.

I glanced at the electronic clock as I passed the living room. Its large illuminated digits were casting and odd red glow about the room. The clock read, "3:48" and I chuckled to myself. Yeah, it was early…she wouldn't remember *that*. I smiled to myself. My soul was stirring, and I was making a little time for my other love.

It's less than a 20-minute ride to work for me and I wasn't due in until nearly 8:00am. That left me almost four hours. I hoped that was enough…my other love is a bit demanding at times. Four hours usually isn't sufficient, but I do what I can.

I pushed the button for the garage door and watched as it cranked open to an eerily quiet world. The silence was remarkable simply because it is so unusual here. I stood there a moment just soaking in the peaceful night air, knowing that the city that will not rest was mostly asleep at this extreme hour. Very early Sunday morning is really about the only time it gets like this.

Phenomenal growth over the last three decades has pretty well merged Dallas and Fort Worth, as well as many other smaller area cities into one nearly continuous super-city. Ten million people now reside in a four-county area that held less than two million the year I learned to drive. Growing up here, I have watched the city flow ever outward…merging with other fledgling cities, consuming them and inevitably surrounding me, burying me ever deeper in its embrace. I like the city but there is a cost, and it's a steep one. More and more frequently I find I am unwilling to pay it. It is the silence that I miss…and the stars.

Besides quiet, this morning was also dripping wet. Violent thunderstorms from the previous evening had moved on, but a low cloud-deck, limited visibility, and a soaking drizzle had gripped the world. Drawing in deep breaths of the cool, wet air, I reached for my heavy leather jacket, but hesitated, then left it hanging on its hook. I simply was not in the mood to wear it, despite the protection it could offer from the chill or a crash in the slick conditions. I needed to feel the wind, I needed to connect with the world, and I needed to feed my soul.

The tee shirt and jeans would just have to do. The vastly reduced traffic at this unusual hour would more than compensate for other risk factors. It didn't really matter anyway. I was not rationalizing or calculating factors. Experience, passion, and emotion were in control this morning. For me "safe" has a tenuous definition and is not always required. "Safe" as many others define it is crippling and unachievable. In reality, there is no such thing…until perhaps I reach the very end of my own road. Dead is probably pretty safe…life, most assuredly, is not. I kind of figure I will at least *live* while I'm alive.

I turned from my contemplation of the very wet world and looked where I knew my other love would be waiting for me. Yeah, she was there, and my pulse quickened as I caught a glimpse of her. We've been together a while now, and she still stirs my passions. I guess I'm one lucky guy.

The gleaming black and chrome cruiser sat in her place in the garage and I briefly admired the sheer beauty and fine lines of the Valkyrie. Even sitting still, the big machine radiates sheer power and refined passion. To the experienced eye, she also hints at strength and rock-solid reliability. For me, there is no question. She has repeatedly demonstrated all of these traits.

As the garage door rolled down I roared off into the fog and drizzle. I briefly wondered whether I had enough gas for the trip, then laughed at myself. I had a wallet full of credit cards and even some cash. There would be enough gas. A thought occurred to me and I rapidly tried to suppress it. As usual, I was not completely successful. The night air called and I wondered if I would actually make it into work this time. The road leads many other places besides work and home and it constantly tempts me to explore and to experience…perhaps this would be the day I would just keep going.

Perhaps…

Despite the wet conditions the freeways were sheer pleasure. Almost completely deserted, sometimes 12 lanes wide, it was obvious they were for me and me alone. Some sections of the highway are recessed as much as 30 feet into the terrain and the concrete canyon walls echoed the soulful moan of my machine back to me. Not unlike a wolf's howl in the arctic wilderness, the sound elicited primal feelings deep within and quickened my heart rate even more. The feelings are hard to describe…but "horniness" is probably not far off the mark. The speeds climbed and I challenged anyone to come and try and take my roads from me. There were no takers.

The uppermost high-speed bridge and connecting ramp of the "High Five" interchange is over 120 feet in the air. Quite steep, it is banked and plenty wide. This morning it was also enveloped in fog and mist. As I reached very top even the lights of the city were gone. The world consisted of only me, the machine, the road, and the mist.

At the pinnacle the gracefully curving bridge turns a little sharper and begins a stomach flipping steep decent to the freeway below. Dropping out of the night into the concrete canyons below at high speed and completely alone is an experience not to be missed. I ran it twice, just because I could. I howled the second time through and noted that the bridge is properly banked for 100 mph.

I grinned as I realized with surprise that the little detour to run the bridge a second time had added nearly eight miles to my commute and whistled softly as the scale of this thing came into focus. It is truly a massive structure, and this morning it was all for me. A colossal jungle gym, my very own playground on an impossible scale. Gotta love those highway engineers.

There are three exits I can take for easy access to work. I was doing ninety when I blew past the last of them without a second thought. My other love was not done with me yet. I still had some time.

Four hours later I was sitting alone at a stoplight with my left blinker on. The orange turn signal reflected in the fog and seemed to emphasize just how deserted downtown Dallas really was. The mist had thickened enough so that in the last few miles it had begun to condense on the hairs on my arms. Thousands of tiny droplets suspended a fraction of an inch away from my skin. I could feel the mass of the water, but was not chilled. Strange feeling. It looked even stranger, appearing in the subdued morning light as if I was wearing multi-colored, prismatic armor.

The stoplight changed and I waved casually at the gate guard as I pulled into work. I turned off the bike and breathed deeply. I grinned as I noted the odometer. My "20-minute" ride to work…something just over 15 miles…had taken me 245 miles to accomplish. It is a long way around the entire city.

As I entered the building the guy working the back desk waved back, and then did a double take. "Did you ride in this weather?"

I punched the button for the elevator. "Yep."

"Man! It's nasty out there. Where do you live?"

"North," I nodded vaguely in that direction, "about twenty miles." There was a strangled 'ding' as the elevator arrived.

His faced showed disbelief. "Twenty miles? In this mess?" he waved his arm toward the outer door and the fog and mist beyond. "You're nuts!"

I just grinned, wondering what his reaction would be if he knew I had come more than ten times that far…and on purpose. On second thought, I was glad he didn't know. He probably wouldn't let me in the building.

Mere minutes later, my errand complete; I sat at the stoplight with the big cruiser rumbling beneath me. The mist was a little heavier now, almost a light rain, but it was warming a bit in the morning light.

Choices again. North was the way home…just a few minutes to be warm and dry. South would very quickly take me out of the city and to more choices beyond. I really needed to get home. There were lots of things to do around the house; there were things to fix, bills to pay, a woman to love, and other responsible-adult-type things to accomplish. Home. Yeah. I would head home.

I looked to the north, but turned south, gunned the throttle, and headed out of the city. I grinned as I worked the big cruiser through the gears and wondered how many miles my "twenty-minute" ride home would take me this time. Perhaps this would be the day I just kept going.

Perhaps…

Cold Shoulder

The humor.

I blame the weather.

For some reason the wife blames me. I can't, for the life of me, imagine why.

Winters in North Texas are for the most part reasonably mild, but like all Texas weather, they can be violent and unpredictable. Yeah, I know I talk about the weather too much, but since my principle exposure to it comes from experiencing all its swings and extremes from the saddle of a motorcycle, it does manage to occasionally become a topic of interest.

This day had dawned warm and balmy, the stiff south breeze keeping the temperatures in the mid-seventies. Pretty nice for January, yes? Gotta love those Texas winters. The wife had her own plans for the day and I had no other urgent obligations, so I figured on a motorcycle ride. It had been a tough week and some time on the road would be just the ticket to put things back into their proper perspective.

On the way out the door I caught the tail end of the weather forecast. The thrown dart seemed to indicate a northern cold front would slide through the area. The spun wheel or maybe it was patterns in the tealeaves, said it wouldn't arrive till late that night or early the next day.

I only planned to be gone a few hours, so as the big garage door cranked up and the warm balmy air rolled in with the smell of spring, I eyeballed the heavy leather jacket hanging on its hook in the hall and consciously decided to leave it. I grabbed the light riding gloves. Even if I were gone longer than I planned, and even if the front came through, the day was warm enough that I'd make it home before it got uncomfortably cold.

Yeah. Right.

As usual, the ride carried me farther away than I intended, the spirit of the journey itself determining the distances, speeds, and directions traveled rather than any loose plan of mine. Errands were run, friends were met for lunch, and the roads of east Texas gladly offered up their secrets to the man and machine flying down the twisted asphalt.

The roads of east Texas have a lot of secrets.

Consumed by the intense passion of the ride, it was two hours after sunset before I realized I'd better turn for home. The wife should be back by now anyway and the thought of her, warm and willing, ignited another, and only slightly different passion. Yeah, it'd be good to get back. It'd be nice to beat that front too.

The moon was out, and appeared just slightly fuzzy due to the moisture in the air from the warm southern breeze. Lounging against the bike, drinking a soda at a gas stop, I straightened up in wonder as I watched the slightly fuzzy view suddenly become crystal clear, the moon coming sharply into focus and the stars, which I couldn't see before in the heavy atmosphere, rapidly winking into view. The shift moved swiftly from north to south. I've experienced this phenomenon before to some degree, but never this strong, fast, or intense. It was a very dramatic effect.

"Uh oh." I dropped my drink in the trash and quickly mounted up. I couldn't feel it at ground level yet, but the front was here, and to make those changes that fast, it was a monster. I was still nearly 80 miles southeast of Dallas. I'd be riding right into the teeth of it.

I wasn't on the road five minutes before I crashed into the battle zone. It was like riding into a wall! The warm winds had been brisk and at my back, making for relatively calm riding. As I crossed the front the winds turned and came roaring out of the north, blustery and cold. The north winds simply smashed the southern winds out of the way and marched on through. I'd guess they were blowing in excess of

40-mph. The temperature dropped so fast my clear riding glasses immediately fogged over.

In shirtsleeves and at speed, 80 degrees is balmy on a motorcycle. Seventy-five degrees is comfortable. Seventy is cool. Sixty is cold. Anything under 40 can be life threatening.

A true blue-northern front, the temperatures dropped nearly 40 degrees in 90 minutes. Buffeted by the violent winds and shivering in the cold I knew inside a half-hour that I was in trouble, but I had made some miles and wasn't all that far from home. Sheer willpower and endurance gained from long experience on motorcycles should carry me through. I could make it.

Besides, I didn't really have a lot of choice did I? Freeze in the saddle or freeze standing beside the road, albeit slower. I guess I could park it and call for help, but then I might have to actually admit that riding into the unpredictable Texas winter without a jacket and heavy gloves readily available wasn't exactly the smartest thing I could do. The fall goeth before the pride, yes? Oh, wait…do I have that right?

Yeah, it's that "guy" brain thing again. No matter. I could make it.

I pressed on. In my defense, one of the signs of exposure (both heat and cold) is impaired decision-making skill. See? I blame the weather.

I slid the big bike into the garage and stumbled into the house even as the door was rolling down. I was *cold!* My legs were weak and I could barely move my hands. My teeth were chattering uncontrollably I was having trouble thinking coherently.

Since I was so much later than I intended, the wife was home and in bed already. I really didn't think it was fair to disturb her, but I needed to do something about my condition. As I stripped off my clothes several alternatives came to mind and were immediately dismissed. Something hot to drink? Nah, that would take too long and I wasn't sure I could handle the needed appliances at the moment. Wake the wife? Nah, this wasn't her fault, and I might have to admit that "not wise" thing. Remember that "guy brain" thing? Hot shower? Maybe, but I remembered how painful warm water is to a thoroughly chilled body.

It was really critical that I warm up, but more slowly than a hot bath or shower. Then inspiration hit. The bed! We have an electric blanket. I clicked my side of the bed up as high as the temperature control would go and crawled stark naked under the sheets.

I read somewhere once about infrared cameras. Apparently the really good ones, the ones that can detect many different levels of heat, have to be cooled to work properly. The cooler they are, the more efficient they are at detecting heat.

I know how they feel. Yeah, I was efficient at detecting heat. I could feel it coursing through the electric blanket, almost visualizing the patterns of the heating elements.

My skin, all of it, was cold and clammy to an unhealthy level. A deep cold few have experienced, and none should. Brrr.

Slowly, lethargically, my body became aware of another source of heat. Yeah. The wife. She was naked too, and *warm*. Without touching I could feel her shape and soft curves, even a couple feet away and under the blankets. Not looking with my eyes, but still seeing her, clearly and unmistakably.

She manifested as a fiery phoenix. Curvy, sexy, and undeniably female, she lay there peacefully. Even in my degraded state my passion responded. She radiated tones of yellow, orange, and red flowing in gently swirling patterns. She was so very, very warm. I was enchanted and with that vision engulfing my mind I gently drifted off to sleep. It wasn't to last very long though.

Without conscious thought or direction, I rolled over under the covers and engulfed her, skin to skin, in a monstrous bear hug. My unhealthily cold flesh pressed tightly against her warm, sleeping, and totally unaware body.

Apparently, it was a rude awakening.

She screamed. Impressively. I'm sure it woke the neighbors.

Heart racing and completely confused, I made it worse by not letting go immediately. Her screaming spawned some husbandly male instinct in my less-than-conscious brain and I held on to her tightly, thinking she needed protecting from something. Then there was the warmth. Oh gawd she was warm! Blessed heat!

I blame the weather.

For some reason the wife blames me. I can't, for the life of me, imagine why.

Ride safe. And be sure and give your wife a hug for me!

Make sure your couch is plenty comfortable before you do.

Storm Run

The danger.

I started awake to a curious tension in the air. It had a familiar flavor, and it only took me a moment to identify it.
It is time…
Can you feel it? I do, and I often wonder why.
Now.
Then the wondering stops, and the *living* begins.

***

It's a hundred miles wide, this scar of concrete and steel. Glistening in the blistering sun, the massive city absorbs tremendous energy from nature, only to hold it ready to pump out again along with the waste heat from the Giga-watts of generated power consumed keeping the heart and blood of the great construction in motion…keeping its occupants alive.

The very layout of the city makes it incredibly efficient at absorbing more of the energy impacting it than its surrounding landscape, the geometrically precise shapes concentrating heat into its canyons and concrete with ruthless intensity.

That same design yields a quick release of that energy under the right conditions. In laymen's terms, the city heats up quicker, stays hot longer, and pumps more energy into a cooling landscape than any creation in nature. The city is a heat engine of inconceivable proportions. Once large enough, and with a violent enough climate swing, it can even impact the weather.

During the summer the effect is readily obvious here. The Dallas-Fort Worth area is known for severe thunderstorms, and weeks of intense temperatures push the environment and the city to their limits. Disturbances occasionally roll in from the west and massive storms move rapidly across the landscape. As powerful as they are, the storms still wither and die as they approach, the radar images showing the system parting around the city and forming again on the other side. In this, the city heat engine has a positive effect, creating what some meteorologists have termed a "heat island" of conditions that the storms cannot penetrate. In short, they hit a wall of heat that overpowers the unstable conditions that sustain them, moderating the worst of the weather and leaving the city unscathed.

All well and good, until we remember that thunderstorms are heat engines too.

Occasionally, even in the dead of summer, a disturbance will be sufficient to overpower the "heat island" effect and allow the storms full reign. When that occurs the heat of the city is rapidly released into the unstable conditions and instead of dissuading the storms, simply goes to feed the power of the developing tempest. In a spectacular display of unbridled power and ultimate chaos, the energy of the city is consumed by the very forces battering against it.

An unstoppable force against an immovable object. A god against a demon. Gasoline into a fire.

And into that, I ride.

Four-thirty in the morning is too early for even predawn light, yet there was plenty of light in the sky. Not the subdued brightness of the city reflecting off the clouds, but rather, to the west, a nearly constant barrage of lightning strikes provided an eerie flickering light and shifting sharp shadows visible even deep in my garage. A barely audible yet powerful rumble from the continuous thunder stirred primal feelings within my soul and I suppressed the sudden and animalistic impulse to run. Instead I straddled my F6 Valkyrie cruiser and backed the big bike into the driveway.

The thunder pounded markedly louder and I snarled as much at my own feelings as at the threatening sky. Run? Ha! Even if I did, just where would I run *to*, anyway? Denied its desire to flee, the animal, the instinct, that dark side of the man, readied itself to fight. I laughed out loud at the quick turn of the powerful emotions. The surge of exhilaration over the dark feelings was nearly overwhelming.

I pushed the start button on the metal beast beneath me and felt her come to life. The half-ton of man and machine roared down the alley and I grinned as I felt the acceleration unleashed with the slightest twist of my wrist, the precision directional control exacted with just slight pressure of the hands and knees.

Power in my own right.

The forces at my command are not at all subtle and I let out a howl as I turned onto the street and almost immediately reached what was no doubt an unsafe speed.

Sometimes I'm not nearly as civilized as I pretend to be.

The streets were dry, and the roiling clouds seemingly struggling to reach me indicated this storm was not yet totally in control of its own destiny. The mixed hot and cold blustery winds told me it was still feeding on the heat of the city. Still building. That could work to my advantage.

The streetlights were all out, the lightning shutting them down and providing its own brand of strobe-like illumination. The Valkyrie and I had the concrete canyons nearly to ourselves. The gusts were getting colder, a welcome relief from the oppressive heat we'd been experiencing. The feeling of impending violence grew steadily as the smell of the storm flushed away the last of the odors of the city.

Soon now.

A few quick turns and I was southbound, headed for downtown on the freeway. The concrete walls threw the lonesome howl of the big cruiser back at me, but that was not nearly enough to drown out the thunder. The sound was of a predator, and it made the hair on the back of my neck stand on end. I could almost taste the electricity in the air.

Now.

The storm broke, dumping what seemed a solid wall of water directly in my path. I pulled hard left as the way looked clearer and found to my surprise that those lanes were dry. I was directly on the leading edge of this particular cell, and the demarcation was so distinct that while the right two lanes were pounded by the rain, the left two were nearly untouched.

I laughed and savagely twisted the throttle. Isolated, no cars visible in front or behind, and riding between a concrete divider and solid wall of water, there was no need at all to watch my speed. The occasional rivulets of water running out of the right lanes were no threat and I simply splashed through them with a "snap" and a puff of mist. Heavy gusts of wind struggled to divert my course but they were simply no match for the power and sheer size of the machine I was astride.

As powerful as they are, the storms are still constrained by the systems that sustain them. This cell was moving slowly north and east. I was only constrained by the fuel in my tank, my knowledge of the city, and the destination I hoped to reach. South and slightly west I went, and was soon out of reach of the heavy rains. I was not out of the woods, even as I headed back to the west I could see more boiling clouds readying for the charge. The conditions were right for more powerful storms to form. This race, this hunt, would go on for over 20 miles.

They were too late though. Even as they regrouped, my destination appeared ahead. I zipped into the lot and slid to a stop in my covered parking space. I sat there, the big bike rumbling beneath me, for fully a minute before I sighed, shut down the machine, and headed into the building. It took all my will to do simply that, my soul demanding I get back out there and ride…get back out there and resume the hunt. It wasn't clear who was hunting whom.

Is the prey, really the prey?

I entered the back door on a tremendous gust of humid, cool, and threatening air. The security guard looked up as dust and paper bits blew in around me. I'm sure the grin on my face was a bit wild as he blinked twice before asking, "How was your ride?"

Lightning struck close enough for us to hear the "snap" just before being stunned by the tremendous thunderclap. The flash was blinding. A deluge of rain poured out of the sky hard enough to completely obscure the parking lot and send drops some twenty feet under the covered entry and spattering through the doors. To the surprise of the guard I shouted a "YES!" to the powerful sensations.

I pushed the button for the elevator and turned to look outside just as lightning struck again. I heard a muffled exclamation from the guard and he moved to close the doors as the wind was holding them open against the springs.

I grinned wickedly as the elevator arrived. I backed in, my attention still on the chaos. "My ride?" I paused until the elevator doors began to slide closed, "Absolutely perfect."

Can you feel it?

I do.

An Act of Dog

The encounters.

I should have seen it coming. I really should have.

One thing I am never short on is confidence. Some call it arrogance. Maybe sometimes it is…but mostly it's not, although many may never understand that. Driven by what I once phrased as a "powerful and devastating need to see", I embrace the journey and find the destination to be more of an excuse than a target. In riding, as in life, risks abound and even though I moderate them when I can, mostly I find them completely irrelevant. I just feel like I can handle most anything the world throws at me, and if it should someday happen that I cannot…well…that is where my real confidence comes in. There are worse things than death.

One female acquaintance put it best when she stated that I just had "a quiet and casual strength". Hmmm. *A quiet and casual strength.* Yeah. I like that. I'm not sure I believe it…but I like it.

Strength comes from confidence, and confidence comes from knowledge…from understanding certain things…like knowing that life is a road. Of course, that is another story. Or is it?

Arrogance or confidence aside, I still should have seen it coming. It may have been inevitable—the universe's way of saying, "Yo! Dude! Yeah you! Tone it down a couple notches will ya?"

Sometimes we need to be taken down a peg or two…shown that there still are things that we do not expect and that can surprise and overwhelm us. Often we need to be reminded that there are forces in this world enthusiastically poised to do just that, and they just might be much closer than most think.

It happened very rapidly...amazingly and almost unnaturally rapidly. Screaming down the lonely highway, I was reveling in the power and freedom of my mount as the big Valkyrie cruiser loped along easily. That's when in what surely would have been a fatal event, I was nearly unseated—almost stripped off my machine by an incident so surprising and overwhelming, that it could only be supernatural. An incident so bizarre that it could only be legendary; it could only be an event stories are passed down from generation to generation about; it could only be the stuff legends are made of!

Yes, it could only be...an act of Dog.

Sure, I was confident. Maybe I was even arrogant. I thought I could handle anything the world threw at me. That is, until the world threw me a dog.

The prudent rider is always scanning the environment for potential danger or trouble spots. Many times just slight alterations in speed or direction can avoid or eliminate a possible danger, provided the rider is alert to the situation down the road and prepared to respond to it.

Target sited. Potential conflict ahead.
There is a pickup truck about a quarter-mile in front of me, and he is slowing.

Risk assessment initialized.
Target vehicle locked on.
Objective is slowing.
Possible Newtonian conflict identified (something about two objects occupying the same space at the same time).
Target is moving to the shoulder.
Blinker is on indicating a likely right turn.
Left lane is clear.
Rear is clear.

No oncoming traffic.
Target continuing to slow.
Right turn probability approaching 99.25%

(ping!)

Risk assessment complete: Minimum threat.
Supplementary information: Vehicle is well maintained and seems
competently driven. No unsecured cargo evident. Texas plates. Male
driver wearing a canvas hat. Large German Shepherd mix Dog in
cargo area. Based on posture, tail activity, and facial expression, Dog
is friendly and intelligent.

It is amazing how much information my brain sometimes elects to collect and file away in the dusty recesses of the mind. It is also amazing what it decides is unlikely, bad sensory input, or irrelevant.

The thing about this Dog…the thing I should have seen and did not…the thing that out of all the details is probably the most important…and the most improbable…

This was a *flying* Dog.

One second I was zipping down the road at close to 80 mph, the next second I had Dog in my face. I mean really in my face! Even in retrospect I cannot identify the exact moment this occurred. Dog appeared just as surprised as I was.

Seemingly of its own violation the plastic windshield simply flexed over and let him by. He thumped square into my chest with a bone jarring impact. My hands were ripped from the handlebars and my arms wrapped around him in a reflex action as my backrest snapped. I was squashed flat on my back on the seat and my helmeted head solidly smashed into the sissy bar. I saw stars. Literally.

I also had the air completely knocked out of me. Oh, and there was the minor detail of who was driving since I was lying backward on the seat and stunned. Dog wasn't interested and it was unlikely he had much experience piloting Valkyries anyway.

I struggled to sit up and grab the handlebars, Dog sliding forward off my chest as I did so. I had to ignore the extremely strong compulsion to abandon any other duties and just bend over and hold my chest and try to moan. Survival won by a slim margin and I briefly examined the situation. The heavy Valkyrie cruiser was already slowing, but thankfully she was still dead center in the lane. I took control and gently eased her toward the shoulder, Dog completely limp and draped over the tank.

I got the bike stopped and kicked down the stand. For once I was glad of the safety switch on the side stand as it killed the motor for me. I was losing the ability to think about anything other than getting a gasp of air and I needed all the help I could get.

Mouth gaping like a goldfish out of water, and still completely unable to breathe, I pushed the limp dog off the right side of the bike and then slid off to the ground after him. I know from experience that when the breath is knocked out of me, the best chance to breathe is to lie flat on my back and try to relax while trying *not* to retch. Fully five minutes passed while I slowly regained my ability to breathe and the stars faded from my vision. Finally I stretched luxuriously, basically determining that nothing was broken, and rolled onto my side. The small of my back ached furiously—the backrest post that snapped was steel and it was to leave a hell of a bruise.

I looked at Dog. To my surprise he was looking right back at me. He was lying limply on his side and watching me carefully.

I have a long habit of talking to things that one normally would not expect to talk back. I have been known, at various times, to talk to cars, trucks, airplanes, motorcycles, guns, computers, houses, software I was writing or testing, cats, dogs, ski slopes, thunderstorms, and once, a tornado…although that conversation was understandably short and is best left unrecorded.

Why stop now? I took a deep breath. There was a simple luxury in being able to do so. "Jheeze Dog. What were you thinking? You nearly killed us both."

Dog slowly rolled to his feet, sat down, shook his head, and then wagged his tail exactly three times. *Thump. Thump. Thump.* He clearly gave me a look that without question said, "Sorry about that. Don't know what came over me. But you think you've got problems? That was my ride I jumped out of!" I scratched my head. Do all German Shepherds have such a strong accent?

I looked back down the road. The pickup had made its turn and was long gone.

"Yeah. That's a problem all right." I winced and rubbed my back.

I slowly got up and stumbled to the bike. My chest and stomach were starting to ache in addition to my back. I was going to have some bruises over this incident. Ouch! The backrest was completely broken off but still laying on the back seat. The metal post was snapped at the pivot bracket. I looked at it with a raised eyebrow, then shrugged and stuffed it in a saddlebag for later attention. My welder would make short work of the break. I groaned as I mounted the big cruiser.

The Valkyrie rumbled to life and I prepared to leave. There was nothing I could do about Dog. A large German Shepherd mix, he probably weighed in at something over 60 pounds. There was no way I could carry a large dog (that might freak out) on a motorcycle. How could I do it? Bungee him to the backseat? I laughed at the thought. There aren't enough bungee cords on the planet. Where would I carry him *to* anyway? No, his best hope was that the owner would retrace his steps and look for Dog once he noticed him missing.

I accelerated onto the road but couldn't help watching Dog in my mirror. He just sat there, watching me leave.

Crud. Friggen big brown eyes.

I pulled back onto the shoulder and stopped the bike. Damn I am a pushover. Women, machines, and pets all seem to have me completely at their disposal. Sigh.

I hollered over my shoulder, "All right! Come on then!"

Dog nonchalantly trotted up to the bike, sat back down, and "yipped" at me. His look clearly said, "I knew you wouldn't leave me."

I winked at him. "Yeah, yeah. Don't press your luck."

Thump. Thump. Thump.

I patted the back seat and up he jumped. With the leather saddlebags, my back, and the sissy bar he seemed able to sit there pretty good. I did a smart u-turn in the road and accelerated hard back to the turn-off. I braked harder then needed and turned sharply. I had to see if he could handle it before we got going really fast. He could. I think he was having as much fun as I was. The bike was vibrating from all the tail wagging going on.

Thumpity. Thumpity. Thumpity. Thumpity.

Dog's face over my shoulder and watching the road intently, we made 20 miles in 14 minutes. There was still no sign of Dog's ride so I pushed the speed up over 120 mph and just cruised. If the pickup truck did not turn off, we should be able to overtake him soon. We would not be able to keep that pace up for long. *The Dragon* is a thirsty beast when pushed that hard and would need fuel soon. Dog was eager and clearly enjoyed the speed. I strongly suspect that Dog would own a motorcycle if he could.

Gaining some astonished looks from fellow customers, we did a quick credit card "gas-and-go" at a small station and then flew down the road again. Shortly Dog straightened up and "yipped" and almost immediately the pickup slid into view ahead. We were overtaking. I let off the throttle.

The road was clear, so I pulled out to pass but dropped her a gear and aggressively used the engine braking to match his speed as we came abreast. Riding beside the truck, I saw the driver quickly glance over at me in irritation. Then he did a double take, his mouth wide open.

I casually waved. He locked his brakes and slid off to the shoulder. I half expected that.

Dog and I sedately slowed, then did a tight u-turn and met the driver back at the truck. As I stopped the bike Dog hopped off the seat and then leapt into the back of the truck. His look, wagging tail, and single bark said several things, "Thanks for the ride. Sorry about the leap...well...thing. Dogs are just passionate about stuff sometimes. Nice bike by the way."

The driver of the truck had stepped out but was struggling to figure out what to say, his sun-worn face working in a series of amusing expressions. He had not yet come to terms that Dog had gone flying, much less come back to him on the back seat of a massive black and chrome cruiser piloted by a 300-pound guy in black leather.

"You," I pointed at the driver and he cringed, "owe me lunch."

Waving at the canine in the truck bed I hollered, "Later Dog!" and rapidly accelerated back the way I had come.

Dog would just have to explain his own actions.

When relating this story, many have asked me why I did not sue or demand compensation. After all, that was an irresponsible act, and it cost me a backrest and some pain. It could also have cost me my life.

All true, but in the end, no real harm was done. It's just not the Texas way to demand compensation for something so trivial.

Besides, everybody knows that Dogs don't have a lot of money anyway. (wink)

Did this "Act of Dog" teach me anything? Did it take me down a peg? Did this incident impact my confidence? Well, kind-of. Probably not in the vein intended though. I picture the universe throwing up its figurative hands and sighing in exasperation, "Fine, just be that way."

See, it impacted my confidence all right. Now I am completely and totally one hundred percent confident that dogs can fly. They can talk too, albeit with an accent.

Learn something new everyday, I do.

Dinner Run

The sanity.

Ahhhhhhhhhhhhhhhhhhhhhhhhhhhhhhhhhhhhhhhhhhhhhhhh…

A four-hour run…just the thing. Nearly 30 minutes to get out of the city alone, and that was the short way (north). Headed west, it is over 75 miles before the countryside opens up.

But a four hour run. Well okay…four and one-half hours. Um…each way, that is.

I headed north to Robber's Cave, Oklahoma yesterday afternoon, timing my arrival for a 7:00pm dinner with some friends. Once I left Texas, I hit the back-roads and added another 50 winding miles onto my 200-mile excursion. There are some nice roads in Oklahoma. Shirtsleeve weather, all the way. Sunny with cool breezes and a few threatening clouds.

Just the thing for my restless soul. Commuting just doesn't cut it.

I wasn't even sure I was going till around noon, I've got way too much to do. Way too many responsibilities to attend.

Finally said, "The hell with it." concerning all the work I really need to be doing right then and decided I was going anyway.

Told the wife, "See ya!"

"Where are you going?" she asks.

"Oklahoma."

"Why?"

I look at her like the answer should be obvious, "For dinner, what else? I hear they have good catfish there."

She shakes her head and wanders away mumbling something about men…or bikers…or little boys, I'm not sure which.

The 200 miles home made for a fantastic night run. I stuck to the majors to avoid the worst of the wildlife, but that wasn't a problem. There was little traffic to distract me from the joy of flying.

Cool and breezy, and still shirtsleeve weather for the most part. I didn't don the comfortably heavy leather jacket until my last gas stop, just fifty miles from home.

Pretty near 500 miles, just for a catfish dinner.

<best innocent look>

What?

The Ghosts in My Machine

The Tao.

"It's only a machine."

Too many feel the need to point that out, the scorn, disbelief, or jealously on their faces creating ugly lines. The desire to change, to influence, to tear apart, to hurt…burning indelible patterns in their spirit, coloring their outlook, and determining their future experience.

I sigh once again. Why do they feel I should justify myself…my feelings…my experience? I only respond because some, a very few, are able to understand. To help even one see life as a journey instead of a goal is worth enduring the many that refuse to comprehend.

"Yes, she is a machine."

That gives them a moment's satisfaction…sort of…they don't really like the "she".

Then I drop the bombshell.

"Of course, she does have a soul…"

Things often go downhill from there.

***

How can a man love a machine?

I don't really. I love the spirit, the companion, the union, and the experience that the machine represents. I love the sharpening of my senses, the extension of my range, and yes, I love the power and the freedom.

I love it that I can dream. *I love it that I can fly.*

There have been many before her. There will be more after. It is in the nature of her existence and purpose that she will not physically remain with me forever. We both know it, and it matters only a little. Someday her body may be replaced.

Her spirit is an entirely different matter.

Her and her kind have carried me, disciplined me, protected me, and taught me.

They have also thrust me into the storm, led me into the heat, and exposed me to the chaos.

I have learned …much…from the chaos.

Her spirit grows as mine evolves. She learns as I learn. With each new incarnation, with each new machine, her influence upon me becomes more powerful. Her lessons clearer. Our relationship more comfortable, less tenuous. The gestalt seldom interrupted, even when we are apart.

With each of my pains, with every loss, for each failure, pieces and parts of past people and events remain with me and my machine. With every joy, with every friend, more tidbits of my experience ingrain themselves into our very core. The ride brings them alive, allows examination, communication, and renewed intimacy. The ride integrates who I am, and who I have been, into who I can become.

She has shown me the four elements; earth, wind, fire, and water, and the additional incarnations…and danger…found when they are combined. She has introduced me to the spirits of this land, not all of them benign or friendly, reveled with me when we could dance in harmony…and carried me away when our encounters have threatened my very existence.

She has taken me places that I did not want to go, to do things I did not want to do, for people that I did not know. Things that needed to be done, and I was the one to do them.

Together we have journeyed to the edge of my endurance, and far beyond.

Restless spirits have spoken to me on the ride. Ghosts have risen.

Yes, I have learned much from the chaos.

The ghosts of my past, the pains of my present, and the echoes of my future, all concentrated in the complicated union between the man and his mount. All blurred by the connection between flesh, blood, bone, and steel. The whole is so much greater than the parts.

Flying, free.

Alive.

Where does the man stop and the machine begin? What is it that the man sees in the machine that he equates with a soul? With life? Is it a soul? A spirit? Perhaps a ghost? Is the machine alive? Or does he simply see himself? Is he reflected in the power and freedom of his mount, or enhanced by it? Is the gestalt a strength, a weakness, or something else entirely?

Good questions all, but alas, never to be answered. See, the only one capable of answering simply doesn't care.

Love is blind that way.

Many cannot understand, a few already do, some will at least try.

There is a spirit, a connection. Some see. Some don't. Some won't.

Can you see? Will you see?

Or have you seen already...are you one of the few?

Have you...perchance...already met them?

...these ghosts in my machine?

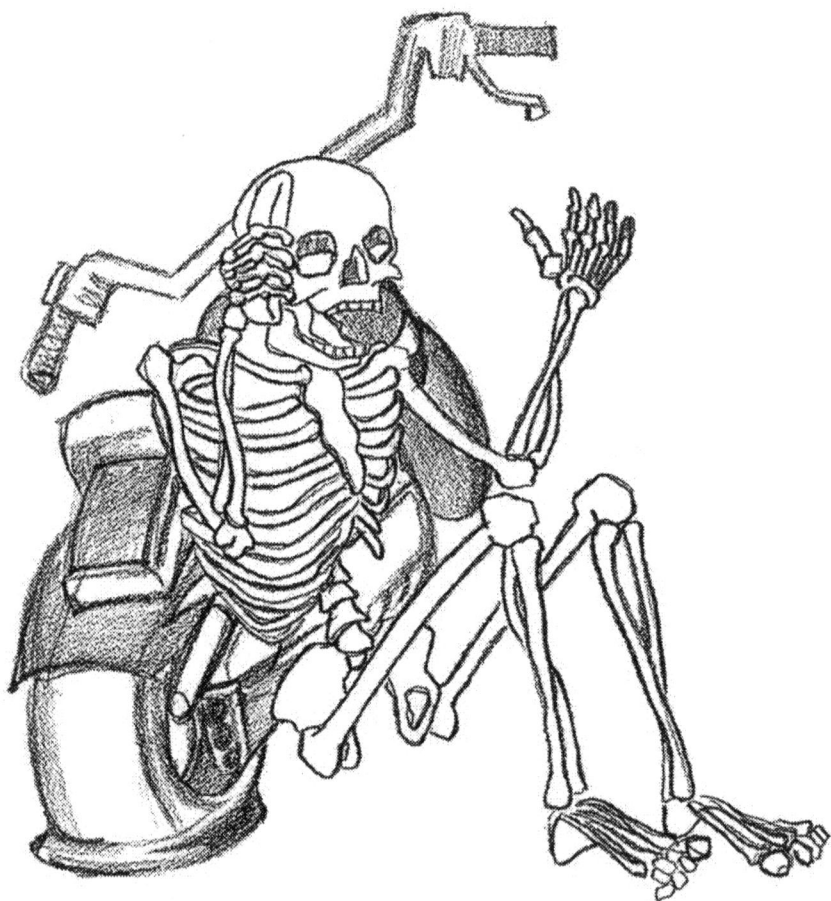

The Horror

The miscues.

You've all seen them...the cheap, predictable horror movies where the square-jawed hero-type guy (herious-pectoris) calls or otherwise communicates with the big-breasted girl (boobus-maximus) and gives her critical instructions. She then, of course does not follow them explicitly, or dawdles until you want to shout at the screen, "Can't you hear that music! Don't go there! For god's sake, RUN YOU TWIT!"

By the end, you are literally rooting for everybody in the flick, as well as the producers, writers, directors, the morons that financed the thing, and half the audience members to all be munched; or sucked, bled, shriveled, disemboweled, morphed, plucked into an alternate universe (ANY alternate universe) or otherwise horribly and permanently killed. They all deserve it anyway...I mean how dangerous can a foam rubber puppet covered in dime-store ooze be?

When the monster eventually kills the last of the victims you cheer. As you finally stroll out of the theater pulling massive streams of movie reel film and miscellaneous bits of projector along with you, and flicking your cigarette lighter and desperately trying to light the putrid mass on fire as kind of a subtle review, the manager just smiles knowingly, hands you a better lighter, and gives you a "thumbs up".

But I digress.

Men and women really cannot communicate. Really! Oh, we can talk, we can throw words at each other…but they just do not connect. Not on any level. Even the emergency "HELP" one apparently…

In the wee hours of Tuesday morning I lost a tire on my motorcycle on my way to work. The massive "High Five" construction zone got me again. Stupid tire only had 1500 miles on it. How many of you spent nearly $1000 on motorcycle tires in the last 12 months? Sheesh!

This is an area where they are rebuilding the intersection of two major highways and half a dozen service and side streets. Some of the bridges are over 120 feet high! The area has been under construction for my entire lifetime. Maybe they will finish it someday.

Anyway, I picked up a major nail or something when I passed through the area and when it slung out of the tire a few miles later, the tire (tyre for you off-shore readers) rapidly went flat. It was all I could do to get the bike onto the shoulder without smacking the concrete canyon wall.

Crud.

Due to some work I have been doing on the bike, and the "locality" of the trip, I managed not to have my plug gun with me. I had the miniature compressor and my toolkit, just no plug gun. Bummer. As I was on the way to work I had my cell phone on me, and being that I was deep in the heart of the largest city in Texas, there was a remote chance it might actually work this time.

I was not about to leave the bike there. Although there are often police all over this section of the highway, all they do are speeding tickets. Any car abandoned here is rapidly destroyed, stripped, or stolen. I had just passed some poor little white thingy that had all its windows smashed out, the hood and trunk pried open, and three flats. The forth tire was missing completely.

Options at five o'clock in the morning are few. I called the wife. The call actually went through (amazing) so being a pessimist, I tried to get all the critical information across quickly.

"Hello?"

"It's me. I've got a flat. I need some help!"

"Okay."

"Bring me my plug kit. It is in a flat, white box on the shelf just outside the door into the garage. It is on top of my drill case, next to the skill-saw!"

That should do it. I knew exactly where it was, as I had deliberately placed it there. The wife knows what all that other stuff is too and should have no trouble finding it.

"Okay. Where are you?"

"I am on the shoulder of southbound Central Expressway…just past the Mockingbird exit, almost underneath the McCommas Street bridge."

That should do it. She knows the route I usually take, she knows where Mockingbird Lane is as I broke down there once on another bike, a long time ago, and the bridges on the expressway are all marked so drivers can tell what they are as they pass underneath them. It is also not hard to spot a 300-pound guy standing right on the side of the highway next to half a ton of gleaming black and chrome machine.

Just for good measure I repeated myself.

"Okay." She hung up the phone.

I waited thirty minutes. Should have taken her about fifteen, takes me seven.

I called the house. She immediately answered the phone.

"Hello?"

"Hi! Where are you?" (polite way of saying "What the hell?")

"I cannot find the gummy things for the tire thing."

She had seen me use a strip plugger on her car once. She could not find those because they will not hold in a motorcycle tire, and I don't have any. Got to give her credit for being observant though, that was years ago.

I tried to be nice, but standing beside the busiest highway in north Dallas watching every tenth car traveling partially on the shoulder until spotting me and swerving back into the road was getting stressful. It is deafeningly loud in the canyon with the building traffic, and I could taste the metallic tang of too much exhaust. My eyes were gritty from the dust. The cell phone was cutting out too.

"No! The white box! On top of my drill case on the shelf by the door!"

In a very frustrating move, she simply hung up. I had wanted to confirm that she found the box and was on her way. I immediately dialed the phone, but it just rang until the machine picked up. I could only assume she was on her way.

Then the cell phone, in its infinite capacity for not working when I need it, beeped, displayed "Conditioning Battery" and then "Discharging". It was now inoperable. I almost tossed it out into traffic. I did kick the concrete wall a couple times though.

About that time a coworker happened by. I turned down a ride, knowing I had help on the way, and still not wanting to abandon the bike. He did offer me his phone and I gratefully accepted. Of course I could not call much other than work or home…all my numbers were locked in a low-power digital hell inside my dead cell phone.

Three hours later (three hours!), in desperation I called work and pulled my friend Dean out of a class and had him come find me. I'd have called wrecker or something, but could not reach any till after nine o'clock. I had even tried to flag one down as he went by. He cheerfully waved back.

Dean gave me his bike and waited with mine while I went and did two things.

First, I found a restroom to pee. Amazing how much better life is when you don't desperately have to pee. I had been on the verge of whipping it out and relieving myself on the highway…but with an estimated 20,000 cars per hour roaring by…well, that would have been when the cops stopped by. They had been passing me all morning and avoiding eye contact. After all, I was not actually speeding, no?

Second, I found an auto parts store and grabbed a cheap strip plugger (the only kind they carry).

Back to the bike I roared. Plugged the tire, and managed to have three more flats getting it to work and later, home. Strip pluggers do not hold in motorcycle tires. A device called a "mushroom plugger" will do the job, that is the kit my wife had…somewhere.

When I finally reached the wife (she had given up and gone home) I asked, "What happened?"

"I drove all over Central and I could not find you!"

"Where did you turn around?"

"Mockingbird."

"Why Mockingbird? I said I was past there!" (Polite way of saying, "What the hell?")

I am not making this up…"Because that's where you broke down before."

That was three years ago, on a different machine, with a different problem.

I couldn't even be mad, I was laughing too hard. I do get the impression that she is mad at me for not being in the right place. Sigh.

In the end analysis, there was absolutely no relevant information communicated in our conversations, despite my efforts to be concise. Words were exchanged, and actually heard, they just did not mean the same things to both of us. I may as well just tossed the phone into traffic in the first place and tried some sort of physic mind-meld.

We truly are different creatures, men and women. Truly different. I wonder if we can eventually learn to communicate?

The monster would have gotten us all…

Why Did the Chicken?

The absurd.

I killed a chicken with my tour bell yesterday. I'll call the hapless victim "Kenny" for slightly twisted reasons of my own. Before anybody writes me to tell me that "tour bell season" was last month and accuses me of chicken abuse (this month is clearly bazooka season), let me just say it was an accident…or maybe suicide. Doesn't matter anyway, Kenny had to die to save his friends.

For those not familiar with them, tour bells are an old tradition for touring motorcyclists. Typically a small heavy brass bell (Tibetan Prayer bell) is attached to the bike low and forward. This is reputed to ward off gremlins and other hostile spirits, and is surprisingly common among the distance-riding crowd. I am not sure where or when it started, or even how effective it is (other then I *know* it works on chickens), but I've carried one for years.

I had spent the afternoon out at the family farm where I keep the majority of my "manly" tools such as my welder and plasma cutter. I had some work to do to the bike for this summer's trip and had let the wife know that I was headed out there after work to "get my bike ready" for a run.

That evening as I was headed back from the farm I spotted, just a little too late, about a dozen fowl of various varieties standing in the road. Here in Texas anyway, there is just not that awful much to do in the middle of a road so they were just milling around aimlessly.

Frankly I figure they were probably standing there debating that eternal chicken question, "Just why the hell *should* we cross the road anyway?" and like any good executive committee they were spending far too much time on a completely pointless issue. Again, like any good committee instead of actually doing anything, they were locked in mindless debate of the eternal question and so were completely ignoring the real world. Ignorant to the last, they did not yield the right-of-way. In the very end...I think...just for a moment...Kenny *knew*.

Normally I am polite and courteous to others so I really did not want to rudely interrupt their meeting...especially by piloting half a ton of screaming black and chrome machine through their midst. I tried, really, but despite the maneuverability of the big Valkyrie cruiser I just simply couldn't miss them all.

KBwwwaaaaawwwkkkkk!   PING...Ping...ping..ing One chicken meets one Tibetan Prayer bell. The bell used to hang from my right lower highway peg but alas, no more. I am sure the bell perked up just as we approached the group, saying to itself, "Man! That's the biggest friggen gremlin I ever saw!" and then, "I regret that I've only one life to give for my Valkyrie. Remember me! BANZAIIIIIIIIIIIIIIIII!!!!!"

Bet that was the first 80 mph Tibetan Prayer bell that chicken ever saw...it was definitely the last one.

Meanwhile the executive committee continued to ignore reality. As I looked in the review mirror I could clearly see the group of birds in the road. The acknowledgement that I had even passed through was brief. As a group, they looked at me, looked at Kenny, then back at me. I swear I could clearly hear one of them scream, "They killed Kenny!" Others responded, "Those bastards!" and that was it. Back to the meeting they went, gathering around the more or less subdivided Kenny and continuing to discuss the issue at hand. I figured the dump truck about a half a mile behind me would have slightly more ur...*impact* on the committee than I did.

Yep, in the end, Kenny knew the answer. Pity he didn't have time to pass it on. I am quite sure it would revolutionize the chicken world.

Later, the wife stepped into the garage and eyed the blood all over my right boot. She watched as I began to wipe it off the right-hand chrome pipes of my big cruiser. With a raised eyebrow she grimaced at the rather large quantity of it on the bike and asked, "What've you been up to?"

I paused in my labor, tossed the bloody rag aside, and grabbed a fresh one. I looked up at her and smiled, "Just getting the bike ready for the trip."

She gave me a rather odd look, gingerly handed me my glass of iced tea, and slowly backed into the house. Not sure what that was all about, but then I've never claimed to understand women. I must've done something right however, she's been really extra nice today.

As for me…well…I'm hungry. Think I'll have dinner.

Chicken sounds good.

That Bike

The obvious.

As I was walking into the building tonight, one of the news types noticed my heavy leather jacket and helmet and asked, "Are you the one that rides *that* bike?"

That gave me a good chuckle…*that bike* was pretty vague, but we both knew what bike he was talking about.

There were five bikes out in the parking lot, which I thought was remarkable given the cool temperatures today and the freeze expected tonight. Five bikes and all he has to ask is about *that* bike…

The monster black and chrome Valkyrie truly stands out.

"Man! That thing must be wicked fast. It's…" he struggled for words, "well…" his mouth worked a moment, "awesome!" He looked embarrassed.

Heh heh… "Awesome." I agree, but I do get a laugh that that was the best a professional journalist could come up with.

As we rode up the elevator I handed him a card. Full-color and glossy, it lists my books and website. He looked surprised.

"You're an author?"

I smiled. "Yep." It's still strange to hear someone say that.

"I thought you were in I.T."

"I am."

"Oh…Surprising."

I just smiled. It's well known that the journalists here kind of look down on the geeks. I am also often just not quite what people expect anyway. Closed eyes and minds are terrible things for a journalist to possess.

I didn't tell him about all the articles I've had published in our newspaper (all I've bothered to submit), or the countless others in various magazines. I didn't tell him I'm a geek instead of a professional writer because I couldn't take the pay cut.

Maybe I made a sale. He was eying the card and mumbling something about "checking them out" as he got off the elevator.

Maybe I'll help open his eyes. Maybe even his mind. Maybe I'll even see him on the road. Maybe…

I really don't know about him…but *you* I'll see on the road.

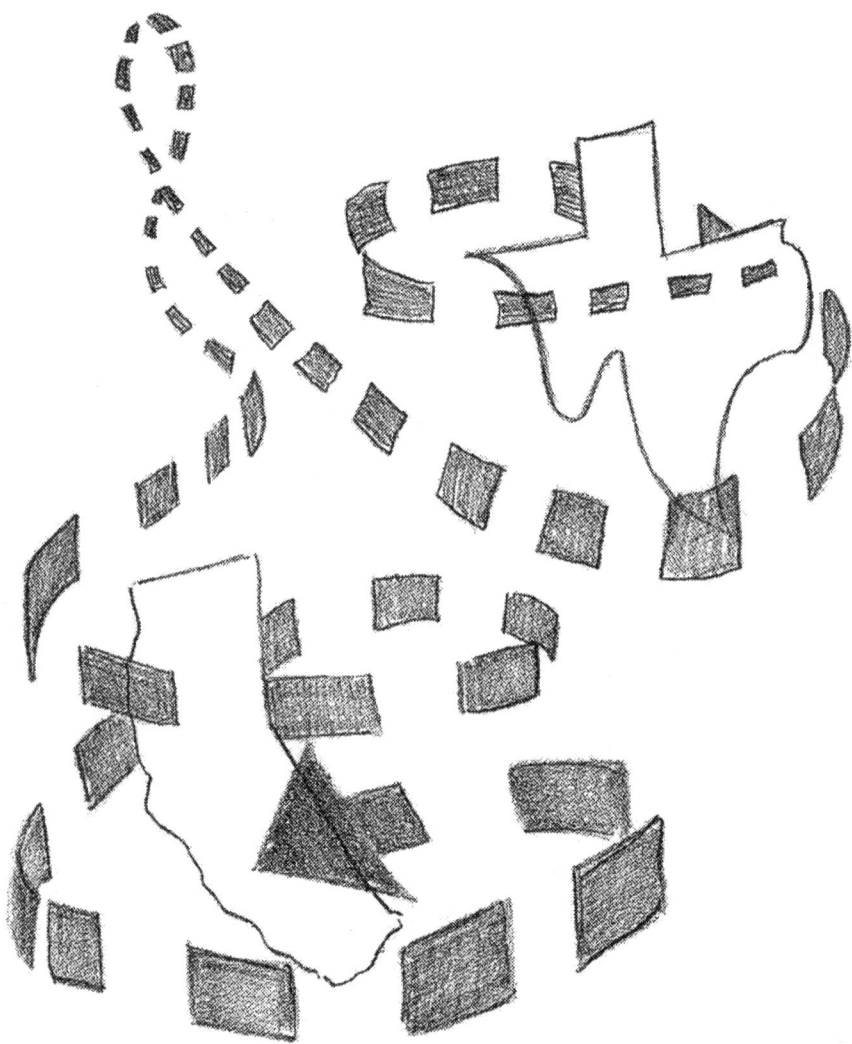

Route 66

The experience.

On the road...

Release, relief, renewal. Vague demands from my soul. Grumblings from the Dark Side of the Man.

Restlessness. Dreams. A burning hunger for experience. The need to see!

The need to fly.

It's time to ride.

I'm headed out for 22 days on the road. I'm leaving Saturday morning. I'm headed for Yosemite...of course I'm doing it via Wisconsin.

Texas to California...via Wisconsin. Yeah, well, I never could color inside the lines either.

Assuming the gas and the credit cards hold out, other plans include parts of Route 66, some time in the mountains of New Mexico and southern Colorado, and a visit to friends in Los Angles. I expect to be at Yosemite for the Valkyrie Riders's event Friday September 16th and Saturday, September 17th.

After that, who knows? I'll have a week to find my way home. I guess it depends on the whims of my soul...and how well my credit cards have held out.

Flying. Free. Alive. I'll see you on the road!

-From my journal

Part 1—See You Again (CUAgain)

So how does one say "goodbye" to friends and family for 22 days? Heck, I don't know. I've never figured out how and as a result, I'll rarely say the word. "Goodbye" just seems inappropriate…entirely too final, yet strangely incomplete. I struggled with words a moment, hugged the wife, tweaked her on the butt, mumbled, "See you again," and pointed my motorcycle north. That would have to do.

Twenty-two days on the road. Twenty-two days with almost no plan. Twenty-two days to run with the winds.

"Where are you going?" my friends had asked.

"Los Angles," I replied, "by way of Wisconsin." I'm not sure they believed me. I can't say that I blame them. I'm not even sure I believed me. That's only the first half of the trip.

It took nearly an hour to clear the Metroplex, the bustling city only reluctantly letting me go and finally vanishing in my rearview mirrors. Once the congestion faded, I grinned, rolled the power on, and rocketed the big bike into the central plains. I was finally free!

I never thought the day would come when I could cram twelve dollars worth of gas into a motorcycle, but I did on the Kansas Turnpike. I suppose I should be shocked at the high gas prices, but I'm not. The miles have to be run. For me, the road trip is not an optional activity. I couldn't feel bad spending the twelve bucks anyway, the SUV at the next pump had gone over $100. Ouch! *The Dragon* will run a long way on a hundred dollars worth of gas, even at these prices.

I should explain the name thing. Riding is an intimate experience, immersing the rider in a level of interaction with his or her machine, the road, speed and distance, and nature to a depth that cannot be found in very many places. Riders are more a part of their machine than non-riders can often understand. As a result, motorcycles all have names, at least, the ones that are regularly ridden do. The beast I am astride, the machine I have become a part of, the thousand pounds of blood, bone, and black and chrome steel, answer to *Dragon*. Some scoff, expecting the name was picked in some macho drum-thumping, bare-chested, alcohol fogged ceremony, but the truth is really much simpler. She's big, she's a beast, and she likes to fly. If I press her a bit, she'll even roar and possibly shoot some fire. See? *Dragon*. It's her name. The big Valkyrie Cruiser came with it. Simple.

Just to complicate things…*Dragon* is my nickname too…but that's another, longer, complicated, and much older story. Maybe I'll tell it sometime.

Seven hundred and fifty miles makes for a long day on a motorcycle. I rolled into Des Moines, Iowa, after about twelve hours of riding. Along the way I shivered in the cold, roasted in the heat, fought vicious crosswinds, and watched in awe the thunderstorms clashing in the distance. A friend and fellow motorcyclist (hi RJ!) met me south of the city for dinner and put me up for the night. I'm sure I'd have been exhausted, except it's hard for me to feel tired when I can still picture the huge blue skies, the rolling plains, and the open road speeding by. Maybe later, when I can wipe this grin off my face, I'll get some sleep. I'll need it. Tomorrow I'll be on the road again.

Flying, free, alive.

Part Two—Friends in Far Away Places

"You're a long way from home."

I looked up at the man addressing me. Clad in worn jeans, a white linen or canvas western shirt, and a white cowboy hat, the older man eyed my Texas license plate as I finished fueling the bike. His gnarled hands and thick fingers told of a lifetime of hard work, probably in the fields right in this area. His battered truck was covered in dirt but looked well maintained. Workers...builders...take care of their tools. In Dallas, he would have looked odd...here he looked practical. Of the two of us, I was the one that was out of place. In fact, I had come out far of my way to be out of place here.

Sunday found me bound for Onalaska, Wisconsin, and fast. I had friends there I was eager to see, and the traffic was almost non-existent. Flying north through Iowa there was little to interrupt a crisp ride on a glorious morning. Well, little except arithmetic, that is.

I had managed to run myself short on gas. Fuel management on a motorcycle is critical due to their limited range, but because of long practice I am usually very adept at it. Not this morning though. Somehow, today, simple arithmetic had been beyond me. I had looked at the map, looked at a mile marker as I flew past it, made a simple calculation on my remaining range, and skipped a town, completely confident that I could make the next fuel stop. Some miles later as the bike ran out of gas and I flipped it to reserve, I found it necessary to reevaluate my calculations. Hmmm. I was off by over thirty miles. Weird. Apparently numbers don't add up the same when you're traveling at high speed on a motorcycle. Yeah, that must be it.

A small town fifteen miles off the interstate was closer than the next services on the highway so I made a snap decision and guided the big cruiser off the lightly used exit, scattering gravel as I skidded to a stop at the turn. Without another thought I pointed the machine down the narrow road into the plains and gunned it. Miles later the small town slid into view. I was counting on them having at least one gas station, as I doubted I'd have enough fuel to even make it back to the interstate if they didn't. Instinct had served me well again and they had fuel available at the Farmer's Co-op. The only catch was that it was closed on Sunday.

Fortunately, credit card pumps had made it here although in a very primitive form. I puzzled the operation a bit, but after I found the box to slide the card through twenty feet away on the side of the building, and finally located the four-digit code to punch in to tell it what pump I wanted (regular or diesel), I was ready to go. I had just finished fueling when the farmer had gotten out of his truck and spoken to me.

I nodded in the affirmative and said, "Good morning."

"Same to you. Where're you headed?"

I couldn't resist. "Los Angles."

He looked at my Texas license plate again, and then back at me. There were the beginnings of a grin on his face. "You get lost son?" Iowa is not on any reasonable person's route from Texas to California. Of course, that's kind of the point isn't it? I am, quite enthusiastically, just not any reasonable person.

I smiled. "No. I have friends…" I had looked away into the distant sky. It truly was a glorious morning, the blazing sun and purple clouds creating vivid streaks of light across the heavens. Finally I realized I had let my voice trail off while watching the spectacle and looked back at him. I tried again, forcing myself not to look into the distance, "I have friends in far away places."

I then told him of my rough plan. Essentially, L.A. via Wisconsin…with a jaunt into Minneapolis and then a trip into the mountains of New Mexico.

He laughed and clapped me on the back. "It's good to have friends in far away places." He winked. "Keeps us young."

He grabbed a large key ring off his belt and unlocked the door to the Co-op. He paused and looked over his shoulder. "You want a cup of coffee?"

I'm not normally a big coffee drinker and I was anxious to get back on the road, but sometimes there is more in the question than is obvious. This was one of those times.

I dismounted the bike and tossed my gloves in my helmet as I hung it on the handlebar. "Sure, I'd love one."

Twenty minutes of pleasant conversation later, I was gearing up to get on the road. He shook my hand, his powerful grip in stark contrast to his apparent age. "If you ever need anything and you're in the area, look me up." He hooked a thumb over his shoulder, pointing at the Co-op building. "Come here. They'll know how to find me."

"I will." I promised as I punched the starter button. The powerful machine came smoothly and quietly to life. As I pulled out of the lot I waved and said, "See you again!"

Boom. Just like that. Another friend in a far away place.

Don't have friends in far away places? Or haven't seen them lately? Get out here and ride.

They're not all that hard to find.

Part Three—A Coin Toss

Having spent most of two days catching up with my friends in Wisconsin, it was time to pack the big bike and move on. The question was, "Move to *where*?" With six days remaining before I was due in Los Angles, I had choices to make. A straight run could take as little as two days, perhaps three. What to do with the rest of the time?

When I started this journey I had a very loose plan. First to see my friends, then I would perhaps catch parts of Route 66, starting at Chicago and landing in Los Angles. Now, the first objective was complete, I had not even tried to decide on a route towards the second. Ah, well, one more errand remained. I would still have time to think about it.

Remember those "friends in far away places" I was talking about? Well, my friend that I was visiting in La Crosse, Wisconsin, was headed for Los Angles too in order to see her very own friend in a far away place. Tuesday she needed a ride to the airport in Minneapolis, Minnesota to catch her plane. I was only too happy to oblige. It's only about a hundred-fifty miles, she packs light, and it was a gorgeous day for a ride. What's a hundred-fifty miles between friends?

A beautiful run, the wind in my hair and a friend at my back…there's little else I need. It was over all too soon, the hundred-fifty miles gone in what seemed like mere minutes. I dropped her off at the airport and with strongly mixed feelings watched her retreating back as she eagerly headed for her plane. I sincerely wished her journey would go well.

***

The bike was gassed and ready. All that remained was the route. It was time to ride, and I still had no idea where to head. Sitting lightly in the saddle, the Valkyrie cruiser quietly idling beneath me, I was suddenly intensely lonely. Where to go? Southeast to Chicago? West to the mountains? There were friends in either direction…more of those in far away places…but which way? Both directions held appeal and yet the pall of loneliness colored the process of weighing the decision.

The heck with it. I pulled a quarter out of my pocket and flipped it high into the air. It bounced a few times and rolled to a stop a few feet in front of the motorcycle. I idled over to where I could see how it landed and without even slowing down as I passed it, gassed the bike and pointed it into the wind, leaving the quarter where it landed.

The decision was made. Heads. West it was.

From my journal that night

I'm sitting on the bed, eating Fritos. So, yah, I love hotels.

Been a great few days riding. Perfect weather, clear roads, and miles and miles to go. Tremendous thunderstorms on two days, but they kept their distance and just provided the breathtaking view...

BWAHAHAHAHAHAHAHAHAHAHAHAHAHAHAHAHA!   (maniacal laughter)

You hear that? That was me, thinking about work...the one and only time I will on this trip. My coworkers will understand...heh heh...

Sorry guys, there's riding to be done. Dunno what you're up to...but I'll try to get enough riding in for all of us....(durn slackers)

Ran about 750 miles Saturday, to Des Moines, IA. RJ put me up for the night, took me to breakfast, and saw me on the road Sunday.

Sunday I hit Wisconsin...La Crosse and Onalaska. 350 miles? Spent Sunday and Monday with my friend Raine, and got to see Beav (that's another friend...you guys put your dirty minds away) Monday evening. I had a very pleasant visit with Raine's daughter Angie on Monday.

Today I ran Raine up to Minneapolis so she could catch a plane to see her friend in California. Now, I'm somewhere in Iowa again. About 400 miles for the day.

For those that are wondering...gas is readily available...there are no shortages and no lines. It IS expensive though. I paid $3.69 on the Kansas Turnpike. It's been around $3.00 +/- 30 cents just about everywhere. I just blow by the SUV's and laugh...man I love motorcycles!

I really wasn't sure where I was going to go after Minneapolis. It's a big country and there's just so many roads to run. I've got 6 days before I have to be in LA. Where to go?

At a gas station in Minneapolis, I flipped a coin. Really. I'm headed west tomorrow...The Dragon wants to run...I think I've gotta find some mountains to play with this Valkyrie in...

Of course...I could change my mind in the morning...I could make the run to the house tomorrow and surprise the wife...it's only 750 miles out of the way....

Hmmmmm.

Sorry for the rambling...it's hard to concentrate with this silly grin plastered on my face....

Good friends, good roads, great motorcycles.

There's not much else I need.

Part Four—Westbound

Blasting west out of Iowa and across the Nebraska border I grinned wickedly at the remarkable change in the weather. Shortly I began to ponder the differences in regional dialects and what they mean to weather forecasts. Sounds strange, I know, but even piloting the big Valkyrie cruiser down the highway under the breathtakingly glorious sky, words and weather were all I could think about.

Motorcyclists, being intimately exposed to it, give the weather a fair bit of attention. For some, a bad forecast means they just don't ride. For me, changing weather simply determines what kind of gear I am wearing and just how fast I can go. In spite of enduring decades of riding extreme conditions that in no way resembled the earlier predictions, for some reason I still pay attention to the forecasts. Today I was focused on a particular term.

See, here in Texas, we use the term "scattered thunderstorms" in our weather forecasts. We use it a lot, essentially for the entire spring, fall, and a good deal of the summer. We occasionally toss the term about in the winter too, just for good measure. Basically, in Texas it means, "We've absolutely no idea what the weather's going to do, not even a guess." I've encountered everything from 100+ degree heat and extreme drought to sleet, snow, and fog under that particular forecast. The only thing I seldom encounter is an actual scattered thunderstorm.

They use the term in Iowa too, except it means something completely different. In Iowa, "scattered thunderstorms" roughly translates to, "Raining cats, dogs, mice, and kitchen sinks anywhere there is a motorcyclist that is NOT currently wearing his rain gear." Iowans, being very thorough, naturally, have an implied corollary too. I'm paraphrasing, but essentially it is, "As soon as he does stop and put the gear on, of course the rain will vanish without a trace and the sun will promptly come to roast said motorcyclist until he removes the rain gear. Lather, rinse, repeat until exhausted."

It seemed I was just getting into the rhythm of the whole mess, which means I was feeling vaguely like a nearly drowned cat suddenly tossed into the desert, when I ran out of Iowa and promptly discovered via my weather radio that Nebraska uses the "scattered thunderstorms" term too. Once again, the words mean something totally different. It wasn't long before I discovered I like Nebraska's definition the best. It's pretty simple, and right up a motorcyclist's alley. My soul and the forecast that was calling for "scattered thunderstorms" were saying exactly the same thing; "There's not a drop of rain or wisp of cloud within 500 miles. *Faster! Must go faster!*"

Hmm. I was headed for Colorado. On my route it's just over 330 miles across Nebraska. Three hundred and thirty miles…with fuel stops and the like that'd be about seven hours of solid running on a motorcycle. Looking into the brilliant, flawless sky, I thought about the forecast again. Seven hours? Heh. *"Faster! Must go faster!"*

I took a deep breath and let it out slowly.

Flying, free, alive.

I'll bet I can make it in five.

From my journal:

Flying west...racing the sun.

I gained on it today. It won, but I gained an hour. I'll try again tomorrow. It's always up for a friendly race.

I'm in smalltown, Nebraska. I can't even pronounce it. It's got a couple extra "a's" and wayyy too many "l's". Great run today, although I dealt with a lot of rain.

I'm afraid I caused a bit of a ruckus in a steakhouse this evening, but I think that's a story for another time. Suffice it to say, none of the blood was mine and even though the local constabulary does know my name, I'm not the one that got run out of town "on a rail"...or maybe that was "under the jail"...I was never really clear which.

Three lessons dispensed:
1) Pick on someone your own size (and gender).
2) Be polite to the people around you...especially the Texan that just asked you nicely.
3) Polite does NOT mean tipping over the table that said Texan's freshly delivered steak dinner was deposited on.

The second dinner was very good, and free to boot.

West or south? That is the question. South (and then west some more) will take me quickly to the mountains. Just west will take me to some roads I've never traveled before.

Hmmm. Mountains? Or new places? It may be time to flip a coin again.

Part Five—It's About the Road. It's About the Ride

Ah, yes, another perfect day. The morning hadn't looked promising. I was completely enveloped in nearly impenetrable fog as I departed Ogallala, Nebraska, but as I crossed the border into Colorado, the fog simply ended. It didn't fade away or "burn off". It just plain stopped. One second I couldn't see 200 feet in front of me, and the next I was cruising in brilliant sunlight and crystal-clear conditions.

It was a startling effect, even more so when I peered over my shoulder at the wall of cloud sprawled across the road behind me. It looked solid, and I wondered what oncoming drivers thought about entering it. Shortly the temperature was hovering in the 70's and there was little if any breeze. I could not have ordered up better conditions for motorcycling. I twisted the throttle, pushed up the speeds, and settled into the ride.

It seemed only moments before the Colorado Springs city limits sign slid by. I did a double take. *What?* Colorado Springs? That would be nearly 300 miles run and I hadn't even had breakfast yet. I glanced at my clock. Oh. Hmm. It was well after lunchtime already and I had lost track of the time. Again. Oops. Hours had slipped by, unnoticed. Yep, a perfect day for motorcycling.

I was headed south to Route 66 in New Mexico, yet I hung a right out of Colorado Springs and aimed for Pikes Peak. I'd say that was on a whim, but it wouldn't be quite true. I do this every time I pass this way. Some say it's the view. I looked up at the peak and found it completely covered in storm clouds. There wouldn't be much of a view today. I grinned wickedly and continued on. No view meant no traffic.

Just a few twisty miles out of town is "the road". Ten bucks and you're on your way up to the 14,110-foot summit. It's a challenging ride, but well maintained. The stretches of pavement, gravel and sand, steep grades, and hairpin curves demand a motorcyclist's constant attention. The spectacular scenery demands it too. "Careful" is the word of the day, but "fun" does its very best to overtake it.

When I arrived at the entrance the friendly attendant tried to warn me off. "It's storming up there," she said seriously, "getting cold and probably sleeting too."

I hitched up the collar on my denim shirt. "Thanks. I'll be careful."

She tried again, "There's really no point. There won't be any view. Those are thunderstorms, you won't get above them. There'll be lightning and maybe even hail."

I smiled. "Hail huh? Well, ten bucks seems a bit expensive to get hailed on. How about half price?"

Exasperated with me, she waved me by, and I moved fast, before she could change her mind...or before I could. No point huh? I disagreed. The weather would do what it wanted. This was "the road", and I had twisties to run.

Four hours later, shaking with exhaustion and cold, I came off the mountain, mission accomplished and still smiling. She'd been right, there was no view. Fog, sleet, cold, and ominous rumblings had accompanied me for nearly the entire run. It didn't matter to me. I'd been right too. There were no cars. There was nothing in the mists but my machine, the road, and me. A view is a fine thing, and Pikes Peak is one of the best, but today this trip was about the road. This trip was about the ride.

I wondered if I had time to run it again.

Nah. I was headed into the back roads of New Mexico. Friends were waiting and I had miles to burn. There were many more roads ahead of me, and as always, this one will be waiting...and calling, when I pass this way again. I expect I'll make that happen soon.

I grinned, pointed the big motorcycle south, and flew into the wind.

Yep, another perfect day.

Part Six—Very Large Things, Very Large Places

I was westbound again, racing into the sun, and I wondered just where the time had gone. Three days. I had spent three days riding the mountains and deserts of New Mexico and it had gone by in a flash. Friends from Los Lunas had taken me in and then spent much of their time showing me around this glorious land. More friends in far away places, and this particular pair have very big hearts.

One of the highlights was the ride west out of Socorro, New Mexico. Some 70 miles into the mountains, on a high desert plateau about the size of Rhode Island, sits the National Radio Astronomy Observatory's Very Large Array Telescope, or "VLA". Some of you might recognize parts of it that appeared in the movie "Contact" with Jodi Foster (1997). The VLA is a radio telescope of mind-boggling proportions. Twenty-seven giant dish antennas, each the size of a baseball field, can be positioned along each of three tracks radiating out from the center for miles. Signals from each of the dishes are combined electronically to produce an antenna with the resolution of a single dish 22 miles across. It is an amazing and impressive work up close, yet out here, somehow it still looks small under the heavens it strives to observe.

Today I was aiming for Kingman, Arizona, an easy direct run across I-40 from Albuquerque, but of course, it wasn't to be a direct run for me. Just glancing at the map I had already determined a zip through the Painted Desert and Petrified Forest National Park were in order. Oooo, there were some great looking back roads in that part of the state too. The straight route was about 480 miles. I smiled to myself, betting I would get at least 600 out of it.

One new worry; I was nursing a damaged machine, and some damaged pride to go with it. An off road excursion to avoid a couple deer in the road had shaken *The Dragon* up pretty hard. Riding the mountains with my friends I noticed that a front fork seal had started weeping. Days later, on my way out of the state in the early morning, the scenario had replayed itself with uncanny similarities. Almost in slow motion I had run the bike off the road again to avoid a bunch of deer bounding across my path. Two hard hits as well as the 80,000 miles I have run this bike were a bit too much for the suspension. Now the seal was leaking with enthusiastic glee, spattering my boot and the right side of my engine with oil.

Why the damaged pride? Well, I am proud of my riding skills as well as the way I maintain my machine. Here was evidence for all to see of a possible lack of both. My machine was hurt. I had let her down. Of course, I grimly reflected, a little oil spattered on the machine is a lot better than the blood that would have taken its place had I not missed the deer. It would stop leaking eventually anyway (the fork *had* to run out of oil sometime), and the Valkyrie is one tough machine. The suspension should hold up until I could rebuild it when I got home.

As I arrived in Kingman late in the evening and with over 700 miles to my credit for the day, I reflected that "nursing" was probably the wrong term for the riding I was doing. Instead of the straight, short route, I was turning left or right on a whim, sometimes riding miles out of my way just because the roads looked more interesting in that direction. This trip was not about "getting there". This trip was about the journey. The bike would just have to take it. Besides, I've been like this as long as I can remember, and the Valkyrie has never let me down.

I checked into a motel on old Route 66, dumped my pack in my room, and asked the clerk where I could find a good dinner.

There was no enthusiasm in her voice as she told me about several chain restaurants nearby. She sounded like she was reading a script. I supposed she was. I stared at her and said nothing. She stared back.

Finally I leaned over the counter, smiled, and said, "Let me rephrase the question. If YOU were going out to dinner, right now, where would you go?"

She smiled impishly up at me. "Are you asking me out?"

It'd be worth it for a good meal. Besides, she was cute.

"Sure. Just for dinner though."

"Then I'll show you." She grabbed her purse and told the other clerk, "I'm on break!"

A small steak house off the main drag was just the ticket. The steaks were outstanding and the bill for both of us was less than it would have been just for me at any of the chains. Often local knowledge can really pay off. The conversation alone was worth the cost of the meal. Besides, she was cute. Yah, I know. I've said that already. It's a guy thing.

We swung a wide loop out of the city on the way back to the motel just because she liked to ride and seldom had the chance. I didn't mind. I like to ride too and this was certainly a nice night for it. She was smiling and giddy when we finally pulled into the parking lot. She gave me her number and told me, "If you're ever in town and need anything, look me up."

I promised that I would and headed for my room, barely keeping my eyes open and fumbling with the key as I tried to open the door. I would sleep well this night, even if I was alone.

My friend was not on duty when I checked out in the morning, but her influence still touched me. I had signed the checkout slip without really looking at it, but as I was preparing to mount up glanced at the paper while sticking it in my wallet. My rate had been "adjusted" and the total bill for the night was just over eight bucks.

Hmmm. What do you know? Another friend in a far away place.

I started the big bike and resolved to make California today. West…I needed to go west. Four thousand, six hundred miles on the clock and I hadn't made it from Texas to California yet! I was only a few miles from the border. *Now, which road?* I glanced at the map. *Wait a minute…Ooooo! What's that? Hoover Dam! Cool!*

California momentarily forgotten, I grinned and turned the heavy cruiser north. After all, it would only add a couple hundred miles or so.

Part Seven—Dream Incredible Things...Build Big Stuff

Oh my...

I knew what to expect, and still I was amazed. Piloting the half-ton of Valkyrie motorcycle down out of the mountains I rounded a bend and as I began to descend the steep grade, got my first real view of Hoover Dam. Amazed is probably an understatement. Stunned is closer to the truth. I really wasn't expecting to be surprised, after all, I had come here on purpose, riding a couple-hundred miles out of my way on a whim just to see it, so it's not like it snuck up on me. Besides, it's a famous structure. Everybody's seen pictures. I've even watched the PBS special on its construction.

Yet stunned I was. I pulled the big bike onto a turnout, shut her down, and just stared. This moment, this one stop, was worth the entire trip. Five thousand miles for this single view, and I'd do it all over again.

I am a builder. A doer. I know what it takes to build things. I've seen the pictures, and now I've been there. The pictures cannot do it justice. It is simply not possible to understand the scale of Hoover Dam without seeing it in person...and it's not possible to understand the importance of the project without taking it in context...in my case by riding through the desert for over three days in order to reach the site. If you've not been out west, and NOT just on a plane, it would be difficult to understand the sheer importance of this structure.

For me, this is one of the defining characteristics of being human. We dreamed it. It's impossible. We built it anyway. Giga-watts of cheap, clean power. The more than 4 BILLION Kilowatt-hours of clean power the dam produces each year—and has for the last 66 years—has kept billions of tons of pollutants out of our environment that would have been a byproduct of power generated in more conventional manner.

Water to bring life to the desert. Power to bring light to the night. Men dedicated...and sacrificed their lives for this.

A monument to the builders is inscribed and sums it up nicely.

The inscription reads:

It is fitting that the flag of our country should fly here in honor of those men who, inspired by a vision of lonely lands made fruitful, conceived this great work and of those others whose genius and labor made that vision a reality.

The men that conceived, planned, approved, and built this structure are truly great men. It makes me proud.

This world, and the things we can do in it, is truly amazing. It's out here. Come and see.

Gotta go. I'm off to dream incredible things.

Part Eight—O 2 B N L A

I laughed out loud when I crossed the California border. Any normal roadmap will tell you that it's just over 1400 miles from Dallas to Los Angles. Piloting the big Valkyrie motorcycle out of Nevada and into the California high desert I'd glanced at the odometer and realized I'd run over 5000 miles so far on this trip. I was still over 200 miles out of the city. "My way" was definitely not the short way. Oh well, I never could color inside the lines either.

I'd expected to be a bit intimidated by the Los Angles freeways. The truth was that after commuting in Dallas traffic, I fit right in. There are some key differences though. One is that everybody there calls the roads "the" and then a number. Where we would say, "LBJ," or perhaps, "635," they would call their big loop "the 405". "The 405" is not really a loop, but come to think about it, neither is LBJ.

Another difference is that Los Angles traffic is on a much grander scale—"the 405" is very much like LBJ, except about 10 times longer. It's also much more enthusiastic. As a motorcyclist I'm used to maintaining a heightened sense of diligence. Cage drivers ("cage" is motorcyclist's slang for "car" or "truck") tend to not see us, changing lanes on top of us, pulling out in front of us and so on. In Dallas, it's usually accidental, the cage driver waving an apology if they see us at all. In Los Angles, it's a contest. Any space more than five feet long is fair game for a mass merge, and double points for everybody if more than one car makes it in the hole. They actually have hills here too, so imagine the extra excitement of all of that on an 8% grade. I'm pretty sure you're penalized for any speed under 80 mph too. I was having a blast.

Successfully navigating the city, I met my host Steve, another friend in a far away place, and made myself at home. The next two days were spent meeting people, sightseeing, and riding like banshees through the LA traffic. I swear that wasn't me screaming in terror.

I was also prepping the bike for the rest of the trip. I changed the oil, repaired the leaking fork seal, and washed off some of the bugs that I'd killed over the last 5000 miles. There were rather a lot of them.

While waiting for parts to repair the fork seal, my friend and I had ridden up to the Reagan Presidential Library to kill some time. It was a much more emotional trip than I had expected. Reagan's tomb set the somber mood and reminded me of the terrible disease that took his life, but the centerpiece was a section of the Berlin Wall. It starkly reminded me that whether we like them or not, our leaders can do great things. I vividly recall watching the news when he made what I consider to be his greatest speech.

Yes, I was watching that day in 1987, and I remembered.

I looked at the chunk of concrete and steel, thinking of the significance of it to the families, the city, and the world divided, and could still hear him say the words, *"General Secretary Gorbachev, if you seek peace, if you seek prosperity for the Soviet Union and Eastern Europe, if you seek liberalization: Come here to this gate! Mr. Gorbachev, open this gate. Mr. Gorbachev, tear down this wall!"*

It moved me to tears the first time too. Ur…well…I mean it *would* have…if big, burly bikers could be moved to tears. *Yah.*

The next stop is Yosemite, over 300 miles to the north.

Part Nine—The Long Way

"The short way or the long way?"

I looked at my friend Steve, "What's the difference?"

"The interstate will cut about four hours off the trip. That's the short way. The other way is up the east side of the park. That takes us up through the high desert and ultimately, through Tioga Pass and Yosemite National Park itself before we get to the hotel. Add a few scenic detours, and we're talking an all day run."

I looked at my black and chrome Valkyrie parked next to Steve's white Goldwing. Both were packed and ready to leave Los Angles and head for Yosemite National Park. Both machines were just screaming to ride. Motorcycles are meant to be in motion.

I pulled my gloves on, mounted my bike and grinned. "The long way, of course!"

***

The California high desert is an astounding place. Passing just to the west of Death Valley (the lowest elevation in the U.S.) and then climbing thousands of feet above sea level, the road showed us sweeping vistas, rugged small towns, and great salt lakes. Huge mountain peaks above us to the west, and desert valleys far below us to the east created views that seemed to go on forever. On several occasions we would round a turn or crest a hill and the view over hundreds of miles of desert would make me gasp. It was a recipe for absolutely intoxicating riding. It was dark when we pulled into the hotel parking lot many hours later. I was surprised to find my hands shaking from exhaustion. It had only seemed like minutes.

We spent the next three days exploring the park and surrounding country from the saddles of our motorcycles. Winding roads, high passes, steep grades—in one case, a published 26%—all kept us moving. Hundreds of miles of curves, granite outcroppings, sheer cliffs, and huge trees kept us looking. Hearty cooking from small town cafés and restaurants kept us nourished.

There is a grove of Sequoia trees here. The largest living things on the planet, they are another sight that is impossible to appreciate in pictures. The scale of these behemoths simply must be experienced to be understood. I'm pretty sure that particular forest is actually part of Texas...things are only supposed to be bigger in Texas!

Standing there, awed by the towering trees, I burst out laughing as a busload of tourists began unloading in the parking lot. Here, in the shadows of the mammoth grove, they were getting out of the bus and photographing the *motorcycles* in the parking lot. They hadn't even noticed the trees. Perception colors experience, and there is a difference in how a place is perceived that is created by how the observer travels there.

Why ride a motorcycle? Why spend hours in the saddle, exposed to the wind and weather, simply to get here? I saw it then. They had caught a plane, boarded a bus, and been dumped in the park. We were in the same place, and I was having the richer experience. The journey is the reward.

All too soon my time in California came to an end. It was time for Steve and I to part ways. He needed to head home to Los Angles, and it was time for me to start finding my way back to Dallas. As we shook hands outside the hotel, preparing for our departure, he looked at me and asked, "The short way or the long way."

I thought about the land between here and home. Hmmm, I've not seen Death Valley yet, and the Mojave Desert is just around the corner. Once more through Yosemite would be a welcome distraction too. Maybe I could squeeze all that in a day or so. Of course, time was running out, I had to be back at work soon. The long way now might mean a long, fast, and hard run the rest of the way home.

Ah well. The journey is the reward. I grinned and grasped his hand. "The long way of course!"

My journal from that night:
All I can say is "Wow!"

Twelve hundred miles of twisties in four days, and that doesn't count the Los Angles freeway system!

Left Los Angles Thursday morning for Yosemite National Park. My friend and host Steve took me up the "back way"...an extra couple hundred miles...but well worth it for the 350-mile romp through the high desert, and then the climb into the pass in Yosemite.

We spent all day Thursday, Friday, and Saturday banging through and around Yosemite. Amazing roads there, and gorgeous mountains. Oh yeah, of course, there are the BIG trees too. Unbelievable!

Today...that's TODAY alone...I ran through Yosemite (and the pass), and then through Death Valley. From 9950 feet to 282 feet BELOW sea level in just a few hours. Temperatures ranged from about 44 degrees at the summit in the morning, to 114 in Death Valley this afternoon.

So, basically, I'm fried....oh, and I turned down the pretty girl the motel room came equipped with (gotta love cheap motels) so I'm intensely lonely too.

Of course...I'm still thinking about the ride tomorrow...where's that map?

Part 10—No Man Left Behind

I was eastbound, and fast. I had dawdled in California too long, and now my time was running short. I had to be back to work soon.

Leaving Yosemite, I had piloted the big Valkyrie motorcycle from the Tioga Pass to Death Valley on my way out of the state. From an elevation of 9950 feet and a temperature of 45 degrees, down to 282 feet below sea level and 115 degrees, all in a matter of hours. Truly, this is a land of extremes.

The hours had flown by and before I knew it, another day was gone. Now I was blasting east on I-40, working to make up the time.

Just outside of Albuquerque, New Mexico, my eastward flight screeched to a halt. It happens—long distance motorcycling is not always an exact science. Best laid plans and all that.

I saw what looked like a very large hole in the highway and moved to the left to avoid it. Unfortunately it was an optical illusion produced from several different colors of pavement where the highway had been repaired. The hole was actually to the left and I hit it head on. The Valkyrie went airborne. It takes a lot of force to send a Valkyrie airborne. It was a heck of a hit. Rapidly recovering I took my hand off the throttle and let the bike decelerate while I checked for damage or handling problems that could indicate a pranged (that's a technical term) tire. The bike was running straight and true. I had lucked out.

Just then I passed under a bridge and caught a glimpse of a single motorcycle parked in the shadows. Braking heavily I moved hard right and onto the shoulder. I'd been hoping to make it to the Texas panhandle today to set myself up for a reasonable run into Dallas tomorrow. This was going to blow those plans away, but it couldn't be helped. I had to stop. I'd just have to push harder tomorrow.

I asked the rider, "You okay?"

He waved at the road. "I hit the same hole you did. My back tire's flat."

I looked at his tire. I carry a specialized plug kit and a small compressor for repairs on the road, but it would do no good here. The tire was split from "ear to ear" so to speak. It must have been a rapid deflation. He's lucky he kept the bike up.

The stranded rider used a cell phone to find a wrecker. He would need a tow into Albuquerque for repairs. Another bike on the highway slowed, but continued on when he saw there were two of us. The rule of thumb is that if a single rider is stopped and doesn't wave you by, you stop to help. If there are multiple bikes, and the riders are not trying to flag you down, then it's okay to assume they have transportation and go on.

It would be well over an hour before the wrecker could get here, and we settled in for a long wait. He didn't ask me to stay, and I didn't ask if he wanted me to. This is just the way it is out here. I popped open a saddle bag and tossed him a bottle of water. He caught it one-handed. "Thanks."

It was after dark before the bike was loaded on the wrecker and I could get on my way again. My plans for the day in shambles, I blew through the big city and found a cozy motel in the first small town I came to.

Yep, my plans had to change, but sometimes that's the way it is...when no man's left behind.

Part Eleven—Homecoming

I put the tools back in the saddlebag and wiped the sweat out of my eyes. The little 12-volt electric air pump chugged away, slowly filling my front tire. A car swept by my precarious position on the tiny shoulder and scattered dust, the turbulence from its passing rocking the big motorcycle. I groaned, "Why do I do this to myself?"

This was my second flat tire for the day. The first had been a simple nail-hole, sidelining me just west of Tucumcari, New Mexico. I hadn't even had breakfast yet. The bike started handling funny and I pulled over just in time to watch the tire go flat. Ugh. I carry a specialized tire repair tool called a "mushroom plug gun" just for these occasions, and fifteen minutes later I was on my way. That tire was getting a bit thin anyway and I would need a new "skin" when I finally made it home.

Now I was just south of Amarillo, Texas. The home stretch. Once again the bike felt a little odd and I pulled over. This time it was a cut in the tire about a half-inch long. Normally this would not be considered repairable, but standing alone in the desolate plains of west Texas, out of cell phone coverage and facing a day's delay and a several hundred dollar tow bill, I decided to try anyway. It took me three attempts, but I managed to insert two plugs into the hole, squished side-by-side. A little extra glue and a little extra drying time, and the tire was ready for testing.

It held.

I glanced at the map. I was still about 360 miles from home. Choices now. Run for home or head back to Amarillo for a new tire? Motorcycle tires are horrendously expensive when you have to replace one on the road. Besides, I hadn't seen my wife in weeks. I mumbled, "The heck with it," and gunned the throttle. I had other repairs to make anyway. Homeward bound it was.

…Maybe I would even make it.

In twenty-one days on the road, fourteen states and over 8000 miles passed under my wheels. Incredible sights and exciting places were etched into my experience. Terrain ranging from mountains and forests to deserts and barren rock had challenged man and machine. The lonely wail of the heavy cruiser running alone for hours down empty highways had once again reminded me of just how big this country is. The joy of new friendships made and old ones renewed was contrasted by the intensely lonely nights on the road without my wife.

Why do I do this to myself? I knew the answer the moment I got moving again, flying, free, and alive.

I arrived on the setting sun, my wife hearing the rumbling bike pull in the drive and opening the garage door. The two cats came out with her. From the backyard I heard our dog, quietly barking a greeting. People had missed me here. I'd missed them too.

I've been asked of my travels, "What are you seeking?" and I've never had a ready answer. "What are you looking for?" has always stumped me. Perhaps I am seeking myself, just the time for introspection and a bit of soul searching. I smiled at my wife. Perhaps, just once and a while, I need to go far enough away so I can look back at what I have. Perhaps I need the wideness of this land to put my own small problems in perspective.

Then again, perhaps I just like to ride.

The wife pulled me inside saying, "Come in! Tell me about your trip!" As I entered the house I glanced back at the Valkyrie motorcycle cooling in the garage. The massive black and chrome cruiser had carried me far away and back again. Together we'd met, and mastered, many challenges. Eight thousand miles. We had done it. Tomorrow I would order a new tire and other parts to fix damage and wear from this and other trips she's carried me on. Tomorrow I would start getting her ready for the next one. Idly, with no sense of urgency, I wondered just where that might be.

As I flipped off the garage light I said softly, "Thanks babe."

It's out here folks. Come and see.

Part Twelve—After-word

"But wait!" the astute reader might cry, "What about Route 66? This was a story about Route 66! You barely mentioned it!"

Yep. You've got me, but there actually is, a point. I rode Route 66, but it turns out that I always do.

When I set out on this journey I had a brief vision of Route 66 as some lost road, away from the hustle and bustle and leading to places way off the main drag. Older places. Cheaper places. Places with character. People with heart.

The reality is that Route 66 is mostly covered up. Interstate 40 has replaced the vast majority of it out west, the remains of Route 66 simply relegated to the business loops through the many small towns along the route. I found a great deal of manufactured nostalgia in these places, most of it made simply to entice people off the interstate for a stop in town. Once I'd seen the "Original Route 66 Wireless Phone Store", the "Route 66 Recliner Center", and the "Route 66 Video Store" I understood. Many of these places were trying much too hard to capture something that they didn't quite understand.

Manufactured nostalgia simply doesn't taste like the real thing.

The trip is still worth the ride though. There are places to visit and things to see. There are snake farms and hometown cafés, museums and motels. There are even ruins—sad, lonely, motels and service stations abandoned when they were bypassed by the hustle and bustle of the world. There are roads to run. There are people to meet. There are also the occasional longer loops where the builders of the interstate chose to reroute the highway. Those are inevitably interesting, as they rerouted the highway to shorten it and go through easier terrain. That makes the loop long, scenic, and twisty. Ride on!

Route 66 is an attitude, not a road, not a route, not a destination. On my journeys, a simple whim has been enough so that I'd turn off the highway. Towns with interesting names, a longer route, a barely visible "short cut", and vague features on the map have always been enough to divert my course.

In that way I've found places and people along my routes that were worth finding. I've seen amazing sights, experienced great pleasure, and even endured intense pain. I've gasped at incomprehensible vistas, marveled at truly astounding works of man, and had nature clomp me firmly back into my place.

Want to ride Route 66? Grab a map and head for Los Angles. Just be sure and turn off the main road now and again. Whim and curiosity need to rule the day. I highly recommend the journey.

And if you don't have that much time, just head out of your city, turn down a road that is barely a trace on your map, and find a hometown restaurant on the square in a small town. Stop in. Order some pie. Stay overnight in a "Mom & Pop" motel. Say "hi" to strangers.

You'll be on Route 66 when you do.

Pilot

The flight.

Oh crud.

I was just getting into it too.

I'd found some little road headed out of northeast Texas into the southeast Oklahoma foothills. Twisty, hilly, and with just enough straights to get the blood circulating, it simply screamed for some spirited riding. Best of all, it was basically deserted. I hadn't seen a car in miles. It figures that the first one I run across would be a state police car.

Flying into an uphill hard left, I was heavy into the turn, leaning far off the left of the bike and leaving just a bit of chrome on the road in a shower of sparks. Grinning intently and accelerating hard out of the corner I had to ease up and drop off the perfect line as the trooper shot around the same corner going the opposite direction. He was just over the yellow and into my lane a bit. I easily changed my line and the big bike effortlessly shot on without so much as a squiggle. My helmet missed his mirror by at least a foot.

Yah, I was moving out. I don't feel so bad, he was too, and I didn't cross the yellow. Of course, I forget, if he's in the mood for some spirited driving, he can get away with it. I'm not supposed to, despite the deserted road.

He hit the brakes hard before he was lost around the corner. I figured he was either about to crash or he'd be coming after me.

Normally I won't make them chase me down…the last thing I need is some kid with a gun upset with me and these guys seem to get younger and less professional every year. In cases like this one I'll find a safe spot to pull off and wait for them to catch up.

There wasn't really anywhere to safely pull out nearby, so I kept up the heated pace and ran a half-dozen more corners before finding a suitable spot.

Parked in the turnout, seated lightly in the saddle with both feet on the ground and my helmet propped on the dash, I waved cheerfully at the officer as he shot by, his tires protesting the hard cornering. He was over the yellow again.

I was still smiling when he finally managed to get turned around and returned. They really should teach these guys how to drive.

"License and insurance please."

I ran across the insurance first in my wallet, so I handed that to him as I fished for the license.

While he was waiting he asked, "Do you know how fast you were flying that thing?"

I stopped, my hand on a particular card in my wallet. Out of all the "papers" modern society has saddled me with the burden of carrying, this one is my favorite. I earned it and fervently wish I could exercise the skills it represents more often. The situation seemed to call for me to hand it to him, but I've always been a bit of a smartass.

Dare I? Heh, need you ask?

I handed him the card.

He looked at it with a bit of a frown, "What's this?"

I smiled, "Pilot's license."

"What?"

"Pilot's license. You said I was flying." I handed him my driver's license. "Here's my ID."

We looked at each other over our respective sunglasses for a moment. He was grinning.

"All right Mr. Meyer," he handed my papers back, "You have a good day, and keep that thing under 80 in my state."

I didn't give him a chance to change his mind. I had my helmet on in seconds. As I kicked the big machine into gear and began to pull away he motioned me over. I stopped the bike next to him. "Yes?"

He looked the Valkyrie up and down. "That's a really nice bike by the way."

Yeah, she is that, except when she's mean and nasty. I like her both ways. I tossed a right-handed wave his way, said, "Thanks!" and was gone.

Two corners later, showering sparks off the right side this time and howling out loud as I throttled up hard on the way out of the turn, I reflected that 80 was probably plenty fast anyway...at least for those corners labeled "35 mph".

I'll see you on the road.

In the Dark

The fall.

Alone. *In the dark.*
Lost.
I took a deep breath and shuddered. There was no point in moving yet. My vision hadn't cleared. Every movement of my head still resulted in flashing lines, vivid red and white sparks, and even cartoon-like stars to blind my field of view. I was awkwardly and unceremoniously sitting on a sharply tilted concrete embankment. At least it felt like a sharply tilted surface. With the disorientation and accompanying nausea I really wasn't all that sure about the tilt. I rubbed my temples and groaned, hoping that would ease the throbbing in my head and clear my vision faster. I had been here for some time and wanted nothing more than to mount up and ride.

Of course, that's not entirely accurate. What I really wanted to do was mount up and run. "Flee" would be the correct term.

There are things for even me to fear…lost and alone in the dark. They're not on the outside though.

***

The ride had started out well enough. The balmy southern night air was perfect for shirtsleeves, even at eighty miles per hour. Running the freeways home from work had been wickedly satisfying, but I arrived home to a cold and unwelcoming house. The wife was out of town visiting her parents and as usual I found the emptiness repelling. There simply is no place for me there...without her. Fifteen years and it's still not any easier. I'm not sure I'd change that if I could.

I threw some food to the pets, took care of a couple maintenance items on *The Dragon*, and tore out of town. The swirling feelings inside pushing me at speed just as surely as the beat of the big machine. Running from my passion, fleeing my loneliness, denying my dependence, evading my own lust, this ride was all of that and more. I hate to sleep alone. Knowing how short life can be, I hate it with a passion that's difficult to articulate. It's tough to sleep without her. Mostly I just don't.

Northeast was my direction, chosen simply because that's the fastest way out of the city for me and it looked darker toward that horizon. In a couple hours I was wandering the dark and deserted roads in the foothills of southeast Oklahoma, the long twisties and occasional spirited straightaway making for the ideal ride, even on this dark night.

Flying, free. Alive. *The Dragon* and I. Aggressively carving through the hills. Leaning. Running. The man and machine slowly coming together until the border between them is no longer clearly defined. A thousand pounds of muscle, bone, blood, and steel...relentlessly driven through the soothing winds by the intense beat of two hearts.

Two hearts. One is organic, a miracle of flesh and blood, flawlessly powering the man. The other is mechanical, a precision-engineered masterpiece of a power plant, blasting the machine smoothly across the countryside. Apart, they are inadequate, incomplete. Together, they simply soar.

***

I groaned again and lay back on the concrete, the heels of my hands pressed hard into my eyes in a futile attempt to shut out the disorienting flowing lines. Blinded and alone, the dark side of the man clawed its way to the surface. Scurrying along with it came all the fears and uncertainties that aren't supposed to bother a confident, adult man. With it came all the worst sort of monsters; those we keep contained on the inside, hidden away from civilized eyes. Suddenly things that normally have no reign or influence on me were freely allowed to rampage across my soul. I wasn't prepared for it.

The feelings hammered hard and fed one upon another. What would happen if my vision didn't recover? Would I fail in my role as a provider? Is that the only role I'm valued for? Is that the only reason I'm needed? Would anybody care? Most of my skills and even my passions depend on my eyesight. What would I do? How would I live? How would I *ride*? My heart jumped. Cripes, is that an *animal* snuffling around in the dark?

The gamut of feelings flew across my mind. Desire, fear, joy, shame, and passion all mixed in a strange and toxic cocktail. I desperately wanted to kill something, up close and barehanded. Almost instantly that vanished and I nearly wept at a horrible emptiness that could only be filled by loving a woman. No, that wasn't quite right. It wasn't love I wanted; it was sex, raw and primal and bordering on rage. Just as quickly that was gone, leaving me gasping. Shame was next. Shame for the very thing that had driven me out here in the first place. Shame for my dependence on her. Shame for my emptiness when she's gone. Shame for my love. Shame for my lust. Shame because I don't want to change it, no matter what society calls strength in my predefined role. Then that vanished too, and fear, plain and simple took its place. Fear with no specific focus. Fear with nothing to fix. Fear with nothing to *fight*. Then even that died. I almost screamed when the cycle started over again.

Yeah, the dark side of the man was back all right. It was all the stronger after being imprisoned for so long. Inside out, I cringed as the feelings, passions, and fears flowed again. The dark side wanted its day. The dark side wanted me to come to terms with it. The dark side wanted its part of me, wanted to take its place in my life. Steadfastly, I ignored the little voice in the back of my mind that was asking me, "And just how the *hell* are you going to run from that?"

***

I ride for a myriad of reasons. Many of them are not always clear, even to myself. Some people ride for transportation, entertainment, adventure, or the social aspect, and I do enjoy all of those, but often I ride for no definite reason other than my soul demands it. I ride because I want to…need to…*have* to. On these occasions I ride alone, indulging my soul's unpredictable demands as to speed and direction. I ride for the solitude, I ride for the time for introspection, I ride for the testing of my skills, and sometimes, yes, I even ride for the danger. There are those that would take that away…they would do so only at their peril.

Deep within the night my thoughts finally quieted down. It had taken a while. Worries about work, uncertainties about my home life, the intense lust and seething feelings for my wife, and pains from my past, all pushed into the dark recesses of my mind, all finally locked away from conscious thought. All contained, put away where the civilized world insists they must rest. My entire being was about nothing more than guiding the big machine down the dark and lonely roads, the bike's soulful wail carrying me through the winding terrain. It was a blessed relief to the turmoil that had defined me for the past several days.

Achieving peace, even in the violence of the winds and the turbulence around the fast moving machine. Peace forcefully pulled from the chaos around me. Kind of like life, yes?

As always, I was to discover it just wasn't that simple. Peace of that kind just can't last. It's the winds themselves we must come to terms with.

Completely absorbed. Man, machine, and road totally at one. Content. Mind and body relaxed and at peace. My being…my soul…all entirely devoted to the road to the point where it was unclear where the machine ceased and the man began.

All that made the impact that much more stunning.

Bang!

It seemed nothing more than a loud pop, but suddenly my ears were ringing and I couldn't see anything but lights and streaks. The horrendous impact on my helmet snapped my head back, causing intense pain in my neck and ripping my left hand from the handlebars. It all but unseated me. In 600,000+ miles of riding I don't think anything's ever come closer. The blow took me completely by surprise. I never saw it coming despite the depth of my attention.

In shock and struggling for orientation I grabbed frantically for the binders with my right hand, even while I was trying to get my left hand back on the other grip. Trying for the rear brake I was surprised to find my feet were no longer on the driver's pegs. It seemed to take forever to get them back where they were supposed to be and apply the rear brakes. I had to stop fast, I couldn't see the road and the streaks and my throbbing head were distorting my perception…I felt as if I was falling over, though I knew that could not be correct, not at this speed anyway.

If I wasn't still running basically true I'd have been tumbling down the road in a mangled tangle of smashed steel and torn flesh. Then a part of me wondered if maybe I was, and this was just what it felt like.

Dizzy and disoriented by the streaks and false images, I tried closing my eyes but that didn't help a bit. The streaks and lights still flew past my vision and now I was even seeing cartoon stars!

"I'm in trouble." I meant it. Maybe I said it out loud.

I figured out later that a couple of things saved me from a serious crash. The first was my flight training. Almost automatically I called upon the little instrument training I've had in aircraft. There is a point at which you divorce or disconnect your motion dependent senses from your intellect. Part of instrument training emphasizes that visual perception and "seat of the pants" navigating can get at odds with each other AND the instruments under low or no visibility conditions. That training focuses on identifying and discarding the bad inputs. For me there was always a specific point of awareness when I had managed to make that disconnect. I could *feel* it. When there are multiple sets of data, and they are at odds, there becomes a conscious choice of just what to believe. No less than life depends on making the correct choice. In that moment, I easily achieved that state when I knew I could separate the inputs, correctly identify the bad information, and safely choose a single set of incoming data to use.

Not that there was much valid data to respond to however…

I knew the vision was shot; roads typically aren't outlined in red flashing lines while doing 360 degree loop-to-loops around my head in time with dancing stars. The "seat of the pants" was telling me I was in some sort of a tight downward spiral—and since I was pretty sure I hadn't been at any significant altitude at the beginning of this mess— that was clearly not the case.

What's left? It's hard to describe, but I could "feel" the road. Subtle inputs from the handlebars and the action of the suspension told me about the surface I was on. Blacktop roads tend to crown, as well as develop a set of tire grooves in each lane from long use. I could almost visualize the pattern in the road and steered the course appropriately. Mostly I just let *The Dragon* do her thing.

Big bikes will run straight and true...and will self-correct to a degree to do so...assuming you let them and there are no radical changes in the road. Of course this wouldn't help if the road made a sudden turn, and for the life of me I could not remember what it had looked like ahead before I got hit. It was like the impact had erased the moment of my awareness immediately prior to the event. Grimly I rode the brakes right to the edge of lockup, stopping the heavy cruiser as fast as she was capable.

The second thing that saved me was that right near the end...when I was getting close to stopped, a shiver traveled down my spine as I heard a voice clearly say, "You're too far right boss. Move it left a tad."

The voice, undeniably female, yet husky and seemingly composed of several interlaced harmonics, was instantly recognizable. It also meant that I was really in trouble, as it belongs to something I normally don't encounter except in dire circumstances. The voice was one of my guardians...I've written about them before. This one was Adoraim, the translucent black dragon of immense power and captivating beauty. She rarely visits, except in dreams...or unconsciousness.

Grimly I wondered which it was. A dream? Unconsciousness? Perhaps death? Would I know? How would I know? Did it matter? The fight still needed to be fought, didn't it? I wasn't sure. Still, I've been influenced in this way several times, always to the better. I long ago learned to accept it.

It is what it is, whatever that may be. It works. I still live. Why should I question it?

I was unsurprised when something pushed solidly on the back of my left hand, counter-steering the bike hard back toward the left for a moment. The pressure released and the voice spoke in my ear again, "Stop. Now. Hard. At all costs." Then she was gone, leaving only a tantalizing trace of her spicy smell behind.

I pressed harder on the rear brake and squeezed the front till the bike shuddered. "At all costs" is a literal term for me. If I use it, I mean it. My guardians—or my subconscious for the less ethereal readers—

would do the same. "At all costs" meant even if I locked them up, even if I went down. It meant something catastrophic was going to happen if I didn't get stopped right then. Smoothly but decisively I kept increasing the pressure on the brakes.

The bike came cleanly to a stop, the superb brakes giving feedback and control so precise that I only felt the wheels break loose in a lockup at the very end of the roll.

I took a couple deep breaths, trying to calm my shaking hands and clear my vision. I was marginally successful with the hands, but the vision was having absolutely none of it. As I removed my helmet streaks and lines continued to stream by, sometimes making it appear I was moving backwards. Intense flashes of mostly red light starkly punctuated the disorienting visual illusion and I could feel the beginnings of motion sickness creeping up on me. Motion sickness is not something I succumb to easily. These inputs were extreme.

I held a hand up in front of my face and rapidly blinked my eyes. Nothing. Not even a shadow. If I rubbed my temples, eyes closed or not, the cartoon stars rushed into my field of view. It would have been a novel sensation if my head would quit exploding in precise time with each and every heartbeat.

At least I was breathing.

Crud.

It sounds silly…but at that moment, had I been able, I'd have gladly traded the ability to breathe for the ability to see.

***

Sitting in the saddle with both feet on the ground seemed safest and I did that for a while, but at some point I realized that I needed to figure out just where in the road the bike was. If I was stopped in the middle of the road, I was easy prey to the first car or truck to happen by this lonely spot. The night had been nearly pitch black. It would be horribly ironic to manage to safely stop while completely blind, only to be plowed over by the first vehicle to come upon the scene.

I put the stand down, and as is my habit, dismounted on the right side of the machine. Dizzy and nearly retching, I moved carefully. My boots touched asphalt. I started to wonder whether I was on the shoulder or the road itself but that question was answered with annoying rapidity. Stepping back from the bike with one hand on the handlebars I started to turn, intending to feel my way toward the shoulder. Immediately the guardrail caught me squarely on the back of both legs, right below the knees. I'd been stopped no more than a foot from it. I tumbled over the rail and down the steep slope. Slipping and sliding, completely disoriented, blinded by streaks and flashes, I wasn't really sure when I came to a halt, or if I was facing up or down when I did. Kind of "three stooges-ish" I know, but cut me some slack. Up and down still hadn't managed to resolve themselves.

This just wasn't going my way. In sheer frustration I shouted, "Shit!" The expletive echoed satisfyingly back through the quiet night but otherwise really didn't help much. The fireworks in my vision seemed to spell out the word in flaming letters with each echo.

I slowly sat up, taking stock. All my body parts were intact, although I was certainly going to be a mass of bruises and aches. Eventually I barked out a short laugh and grinned ruefully. At least I knew the bike was parked on the shoulder!

"Damn."

I got unsteadily to my feet and carefully made my way up the hill. Shortly I should have found the guardrail and the bike, but after going what I was sure was too far I halted, confused. I turned to my right, somehow deciding that was the correct direction and intending on walking a few paces parallel to the slope. I stopped when I realized I was walking on steeply sloped concrete instead of rock and grass. I was startled to realize I didn't know how long ago the surface had changed or even how long I'd actually been walking.

A little bit of sense finally poked its way through the disorientation and one of the first rules of how to behave if lost popped into my head. Basically, I needed to just stop. Wandering around aimlessly just makes it worse, leading to possible injury at the worst, and at the very best, just more…ur…uh…lostness. Yeah.

With a sigh I slumped down on the concrete slope. I needed help and I knew it. That's not an easy thing for me to realize. I pulled my cell phone out of my back pocket and unlocked the keys by feel. I thumbed down a few entries in my phonebook, not sure of who it landed on. I knew that anybody in the index that I could reach would know me and be able to at least get the proper help to call me back. I pushed the "call" button and put the thing to my ear.

Shortly the phone beeped three times. The call wouldn't go through. Typical. I tried again with the same result. I guessed the three beeps meant there was no service out here, but with nothing else productive to do I kept trying.

When I realized it was futile an uncharacteristically strong surge of emotion shot through me. I had the overwhelming urge to throw the phone as far as I could. Surprised, I realized my hands were shaking and made a conscious effort to calm down. I was only partially successful. The first of my demons was coming to visit me.

I locked the keys again and stuffed the cell phone back in my pocket. My disorientation cost me again, as I did not get it fully in the pocket and as I slewed back around to put my hands on my knees I heard the phone go sliding and skipping down the concrete slope. It seemed to go rather a long way. I never heard it hit the bottom.

Alone. *In the dark.*

Lost.

***

Old lovers, old pains. Failures. Demons. Scars. We all have them. We're rarely put in a position where they can freely come to visit. Civilized life demands we hide them away, that we keep them from close examination. We're rarely prepared to face them down.

As the waves of dizziness were accompanied by emotions and vivid memories too powerful to fend off, I found myself straining to look upward. *If I could just see the stars...*

This was going to be a long night.

Demons, failures, scars. It doesn't matter what they're called. One by one they rolled on through my soul, exposing the fears and failures, prodding the raw pains of lost lovers and missing friends, and replaying all the times I made choices I knew were wrong. One by one they rejoiced in the pain they caused, never realizing that in being forced to face them, I was slowly coming to terms with them. Never realizing that their true power only lay in the fact that I'd not consciously done so in the past. Never realizing that, as a part of me, as a creation of my own id, as a manifestation of my own dark side, that they could not destroy me in the process. Despite the pain I knew they could only make me stronger, more complete. What does not kill me makes me stronger, yes?

Eventually exhaustion overtook me and I gratefully drifted off to sleep. As I fell into the darkness I thought I heard a large animal moving nearby again. Before I started fully awake in alarm I felt the distinct and unmistakable presence of my guardians return, one of them, the wolf this time—large and warm and furry and perfect to hold onto—nestled tightly against my side.

"We've got you boss. Sleep."

***

The bare glimmerings of early predawn light woke me and I sat up blinking at the purple and black sky and wondering where I was. It took fully two minutes before the memories came back and I realized the weak light had awakened me because I could see it.

I could see!

I was sitting on the sloped concrete erosion control structure of a bridge, far below the road and on the other side of it from my bike. Apparently I had actually crossed under the bridge in my directionless and disoriented wandering around. It was a good 40 feet down the sloping concrete to a mostly dry riverbed below. What water remained was running in a narrow central channel.

I shuffled straight down the concrete until it ended on the dirt bed and looked around for my phone. It wasn't hard to find, and I brushed the dirt off it and thumbed the keys. Through the cracked display I could see that I had been correct earlier. It had no signal. They just don't put cell towers along the back roads of America. I grinned. I can't really gripe. That's one of the reasons I ride them I guess.

It was a long climb back up to the bike, and once again I resolved to get in better shape. The bike was parked on the shoulder, less than a foot from the side guardrail. A chill shot through me as I saw that the front tire was stopped not more than six inches from impacting the concrete railing where the road narrowed to cross the bridge. My eyes traced the trajectory my body would have taken had I hit that at speed and I blinked at the sheer height of the bridge when viewed with that criteria. "At all costs" indeed.

A quick inspection of the bike revealed no major damage. The windshield was deeply scratched near the top left side and would need to be replaced. That was a clue to the nature and strength of the impact. Those windshields are very hard to scratch deeply. My helmet was deeply scarred on the left chin covering and over the top just above my left eye. The face shield was completely gone, ripped away along with one of the pivot points (called base plates). The clear riding glasses I'd been wearing had been ripped off my face, the tough polycarbonate lenses nowhere to be found. I found myself looking at the deep abrasion patterns on the helmet and wondering if I would even have eyes had I not been wearing the glasses. I'd guess without the helmet I'd have been scalped. Hmmm. It was useful for once. I usually wear it simply to keep my earphones in. Heh.

The abrasions and obvious weight of the impact convinced me it was a "road gator", the motorcyclist's slang for those big truck tire treads left in the road after a blow out. They are heavy and solid, and usually have steel cords sticking out of them to do all sorts of nasty damage. They normally don't hover though…this one had caught me at head level. It must have been thrown up by a truck, but I didn't remember passing one. That's okay though. I didn't remember seeing anything about to hit me either.

Those memories are probably hanging out with the shattered remains of my glasses, wherever it is they ended up.

I looked behind the bike for debris, but it was too dark to see very far against the black road surface and I couldn't spot anything. I shrugged. Irrelevant anyway. Life rolls forward.

I'd left the ignition key on, and the bike's lights were very dim. I turned it off, wondering whether the battery had sufficient power to start the bike. I looked around at the barely visible countryside and shrugged. I may as well give it a try.

I saddled up, put on my helmet, and fished around in my tank bag for some more glasses. Sunglasses were the best I could do, but I chose the lightest colored pair I had. With no face shield, tinted lenses were better than nothing.

The starter wouldn't turn the engine, but I knew how to handle that. The sheer weight of the Valkyrie actually makes her easier to push start, provided there is enough juice for the ignition to fire. Well, that and if the road is not uphill. There was only one way to find out if she'd start. I backed the bike off the shoulder, pointed her over the bridge, popped her into third, and rocked forward, letting the clutch briefly and partially out just as I reached the end of the push and my feet came off the ground. I pulled the clutch back in as the big engine came to life, popping slightly. I watched the voltage gauge climb as the alternator began feeding the hungry battery. Shortly *The Dragon* was running smoothly.

I sighed in relief. "Thanks babe."

As I worked the big bike through her gears I pondered my destination. I was far into the back roads, perhaps 80 miles southeast of McAlester, Oklahoma. Behind me, not too far, was the Arkansas border. My vision was still a bit shaky, pulses of light throbbing in time with my heart when I exerted myself very hard. I decided to head for McAlester. It's a big enough town that I was sure I could find medical care there.

***

Gently carving corners, totally absorbed in the road, the cool winds managed to blow the last dregs of my ordeal from my mind. Within 30 miles I was totally refreshed, reveling in the power available with the slight twist of my wrist, the big machine nimbly responding to my every whim. *Ahhhh.*

I really do love to ride.

My mind turned to the thoughts and emotions from the night before, and I smiled and twisted the throttle even more, laughing to the winds. Yes, I have a dark side. Yes, I have my failures and my pains. The dark side is integral and necessary; I'd simply been pushing it down too far. Society seems to demand it and I'd been wrong to allow it. The fight, the aggression, the passion, the *drive*…all are necessary to some degree. Suppressing it does nothing positive, and indeed, gives it power it does not deserve and should not wield. My failures and pains came to haunt me, but one by one were balanced out by my successes and my pleasures. One by one they came to kill or enslave me, and one by one they lost their power and died, snuffed out by the very act of their own exposure.

I howled as I negotiated one particularly tight turn, accelerating uphill into the barely visible landscape, the fresh air reviving both my body and spirit. Without realizing it I'd changed my plans. Medical attention? Bah. Breakfast was what I really needed. A big one. It'd be more effective and a hell of a lot cheaper. Then I had to get to work. At a guess it was a couple hundred miles to Dallas. With any luck and a little bit of speed, I might even make it before rush hour.

With a savage joy I turned my thoughts once again to the road and the precision machine I was astride, its lonely wail carrying me through the remains of the night.

The dark side of the man. It's a primal, powerful, and sometimes dangerous thing, but we've still got to let it out once and a while. I've met mine, and though I wouldn't say I've conquered it, I at least know that when it's necessary that I set it free, it will do my bidding.

More or less. Sometimes. *Mostly.*

The day may come when my dark side again gains more power than it should. The day may come when unbidden, my dark side claws its way to the surface and sets its sights on me. The day may come when I see its unpleasant grin again. Yeah, that day will arrive. When it does, and the dark side rises, I'll meet its eyes, plant my feet, grin, and say, "Bring it."

As for my failures, my pains, and my demons, well, they all have their counterpart. I've successes, pleasures, and guardians. Life will be what I make of it, and I've all the aces on my side.

I think I'll watch out for the friggen road gators though.

***

Alone. In the dark.
Lost.
There *are* scary things.
But the scary things aren't on the outside…
What is it that you see, alone, in the dark?

Conclusion

Another night. Another run. Another winter storm. I pulled the big cruiser into the garage and stepped back out into the driveway, exhaling and watching the expanding cloud of my condensing breath in the predawn light. In the garage, *The Dragon* began popping and hissing as the heat from the engine melted ice that had managed to freeze to her while we were moving. The drips vaporized with a snap and a sizzle each time they landed on the exhaust.

Cold weather usually depresses me. I prefer the heat of the Texas summer, and yet, there's a strange attraction to the unpredictability of our usually mild winter conditions. In fact, even now the sky was clear and I'd been out of the sleet for miles. Even with the lights of the city, and the dawn breaking to the east, I could still see stars to the west. That's unusual here. Arms spread wide and exhaling another cloud of crystallized breath, I looked up at the magnificent sky and grinned.

"Good morning," my wife said dryly.

Not the least chagrined, I dropped my arms and turned toward her voice. She'd heard me arrive and was leaning against the door that led from the garage into the house. I hadn't heard her open it.

Clad only in a thin, light tee shirt, even in the dim light she was all enticing shapes, revealing shadows, and soft curves. I caught my breath. All this time, and still my desire for her is unabashedly just as strong or stronger as when we were first together. Damn that male brain anyway. If only it could be harnessed for something useful.

Not moving from my spot in the driveway, I leered at her, "Hey lover."

"How was your trip?"

I took a deep breath and let it out again, watching the steam fly. "Perfect."

She glanced significantly at the bike, the ice still melting and sizzling away. She looked back at me with a raised eyebrow. "You look like you could use a hot shower."

I peered down at my heavy leather jacket. Instead of black, it shone nearly white with a coating of light frost. It was dimpled with heavier frozen droplets stuck all over in random patterns. The ice was thick enough that it partially obscured the brilliant red dragon embroidered on the front of the jacket. Winking, I thumped myself across the chest with one arm and pretended to ignore the smattering of ice particles that fell and bounced around my feet on the cold pavement. "It's not so bad."

She smiled, "Come on. The shower will do you good. I'll join you."

I leered again. "Now you're talking." I looked at the sky again. "You go get it started. I'll be right there." A new day was coming. There was something I had to do.

"All right. Don't be too long." She smiled suggestively and closed the door.

The light to the east was much brighter. Like a wave, the sun was about to break over the fences and houses that were blocking my view of its daily rebirth.

This ride, like many, had challenged man and machine. Skill, reliability, experience, and confidence had been put to the test, and with just a smattering of luck, had passed it with flying colors. Another experience earned. Another unexpected danger faced down and dealt with. Another bit of knowledge to help me the next time. Another time that I found my way. Another reward at the end of the journey.

Kind of like life, yes?

The sky flared brightly as the sunlight flowed over everything in its path. Raising my arms again I faced the east and closed my eyes, sensing the dazzling brilliance with the feeling of warmth on my face instead of simply watching with my eyes.

It had been a long night…a long ride. I took a deep breath and let it out slowly.

Why do I do this? There are times I have trouble answering that question, but yes, I do know. It's about the experiences along my path. It's about the sights and smells. It's about the magic to be found in this world for those of us that know how to seek it. It's about encounters with the other souls seeking their path, while we strive to find our own. It's about simple pleasures. And sometimes, yes, it's even about the danger and the pain.

It's about the sunrise. It's about another day. It's about a lot of things…but it's not really about *life*. It's about *living*.

It's about the ride.

The kiss of the sun on my face sent a shiver of pleasure up my spine, a wonderful contrast from what I'd endured that night. Slowly I opened my eyes. A new day was here. A new ride loomed ahead. New experiences waited. New challenges and pleasures lay before me, some of them right *here*.

I thought of her, warm and willing and waiting just for me, and dropped my arms to my sides.

Without looking back I headed into the house. As the big garage door rumbled down, I thought of her once more and my heart quickened.

Yeah. It was a new day. A new experience. A new ride. It was all waiting…and *she* was waiting, the hot shower already steaming up the room.

Yep. A new day to ride. A new day to love. A new day to *live*.

I grinned and said quietly, "I guess I'd better get started."

I'll see you on the road.

Also available at www.lifeisaroad.com or your favorite bookseller

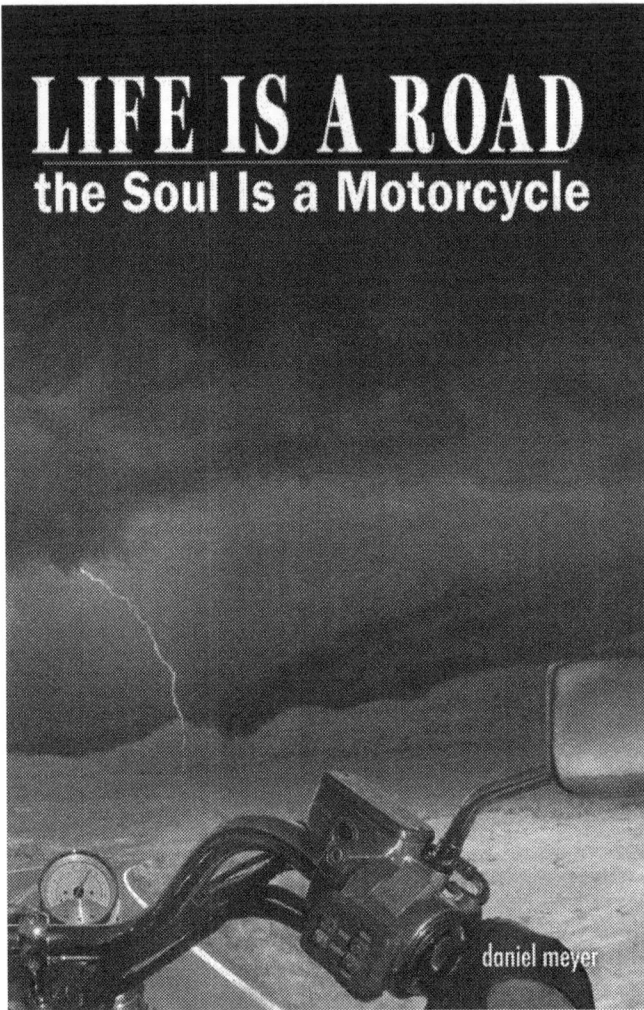

LIFE IS A ROAD
the Soul Is a Motorcycle

daniel meyer

Life Is a Road, the Soul Is a Motorcycle

Cresting the hill, something caught my eye and I became suddenly alert.

Oh my . . .

Join the author in a series of adventures as he rediscovers what he had known deep in his soul all along—experience is the purpose, the journey is the destination.

Life Is a Road, Get On it and Ride!

Join the author as he narrates with humor and passion a fantastic series of adventures as he rediscovers what he had known deep in his soul all along—experience is the purpose, the journey is the destination, and indeed, that *life is a road.*

"A little bit of Jung, a little bit of Freud, and a little bit of rock and roll." (Doc D)

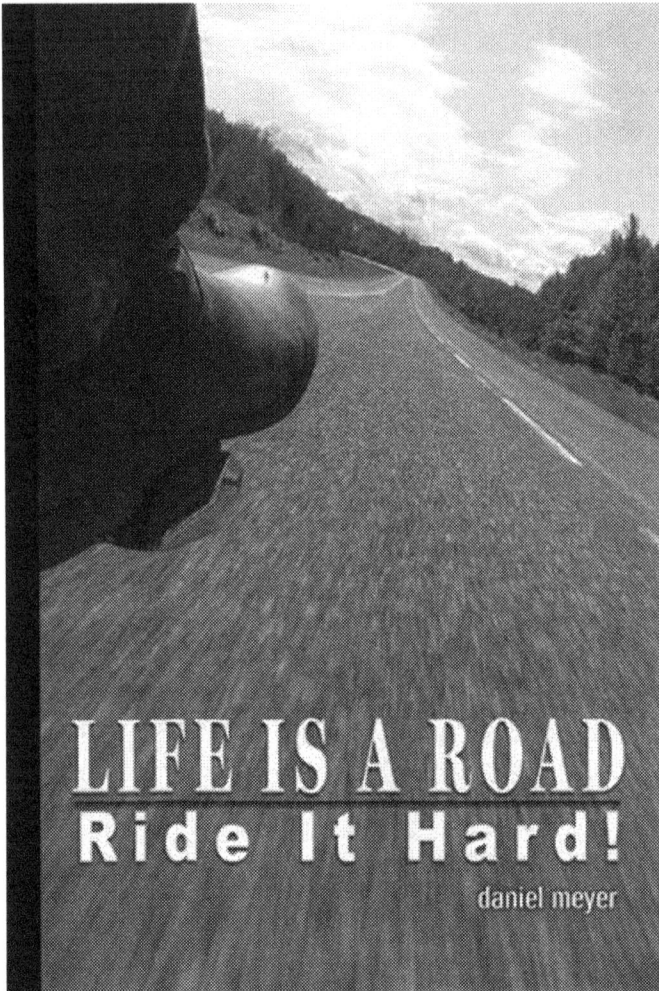

Life Is a Road, Ride It Hard!

10,158 miles. Incredible thunderstorms, raging forest fires, dense smoke, hail, sleet, cops, a half-a-dozen paramedics, bears, and even a dragon or two…you know…the usual stuff.

Ride the Alaskan Highway all the way there and back again. It's 4365 miles each way, Dallas to Fairbanks…

Coming from Storm Rider Press and Daniel Meyer in 2007:

The gods of old walk the earth in human form. Some of them aren't happy about it...and some of them don't know.

Storm Rider

A full-length motorcycle fiction novel.

Watch for it at www.lifeisaroad.com and www.stormriderpress.com